Living Better with Spirituality Based Strategies that Work

Living Better with Spirituality Based Strategies that Work

Workbook for Spiritually Informed Therapy

Thomas G. Plante, PhD, ABPP

Santa Clara University | Stanford University School of Medicine

Bassim Hamadeh, CEO and Publisher
Amy Smith, Senior Project Editor
Abbey Hastings, Production Editor
Emely Villavicencio, Senior Graphic Designer
Kylie Bartolome, Licensing Coordinator
Natalie Piccotti, Director of Marketing
Kassie Graves, Senior Vice President, Editorial
Jamie Giganti, Director of Academic Publishing

Cover image: Copyright © 2009 iStockphoto LP/lopurice.

Printed in the United States of America.

Parts of this book are taken from Thomas Plante, *Spiritually Informed Therapy: Wisdom and Evidence Based Strategies that Work*. Copyright © 2023 by Cognella, Inc. Reprinted with permission.

320 South Cedros Ave., Ste. 400, Solana Beach, CA 92075

Ad Maiorem Dei Gloriam

Brief Contents

Contents

Preface

Every now and then, someone or some group seems to rediscover a strategy from the great wisdom traditions that can be used for the benefit of diverse contemporary people. Mindfulness and yoga are both good examples as they come from ancient spiritual and religious traditions but have been rediscovered in more recent years and successfully adapted for general and secular audiences. Yet perhaps mindfulness and yoga are merely just the tip of the iceberg. There are so many additional strategies for better living that come from the religious and spiritual traditions waiting to be rediscovered and translated into contemporary use for better living.

This book seeks to help with this rediscovering process by highlighting Jesuit spirituality and strategies and incorporating them into secular and spiritually informed life principles. The book highlights cornerstone principles used for over 500 years in Jesuit spirituality and then translates them for contemporary times and for general audiences. These principles include seeing God (or the sacred) in all things; caring for the whole person (i.e., *cura personalis*); using a pathway for decision-making focusing on discernment; ending the day with a five-step reflection (i.e., the Examen); managing conflicts with accommodation, humility, and the expectation for goodness; developing a pathway for achieving kinship with others; and so forth. The book also provides many brief examples of how these life principles can be used with diverse populations and situations as well. These examples are real-life cases, but names and details have been carefully altered to maintain confidentiality. One book certainly cannot address all that needs to be addressed in offering spiritual informed life principles highlighting Jesuit spirituality. The concluding chapter offers further reading and strategies to pursue this topic for interested readers.

In my 30 years working at a Jesuit university and conducting spiritual informed therapy with my own clinical clients in private practice, I have concluded that Jesuit spirituality, and the religious and spiritual traditions more generally, have so much to offer. If we look carefully and without bias, we can see the riches of strategies, principles, and interventions to add to our life management toolbox that will likely ultimately make us all better people and more satisfied and happy too. I hope that this book is a step in the right direction for you in doing so.

Thomas G. Plante, PhD, ABPP
Santa Clara University and
Stanford University School of Medicine
June 2023

Acknowledgments

I am grateful to Santa Clara University and the Jesuits there as well as others who have informed my thinking about spiritually informed therapy for over 30 years. Additionally, I am grateful to all those who assisted me with this project. First, I am grateful to Kassie Graves from Cognella, who graciously and enthusiastically expressed interest in this project and offered a book contract shortly after our initial meeting to discuss my ideas. Additionally, I am also grateful to the other terrific professionals at Cognella, including Amy Smith, Abbey Hastings, and Rachel Kahn. I am grateful to friend and running partner Deacon John Kerrigan, who enthusiastically suggested writing this workbook. I am grateful to my wife, Lori Plante, who edited and corrected earlier versions of the manuscript. We have been a wonderful team in multiple ways both personally and professionally for over 40 years. Finally, Lori and my son, Zach, are daily blessings in my life for which I am eternally grateful.

CHAPTER 1

Introduction

What Are Spiritually Informed Life Principles?

Case Examples Lydia, Jake, and Adam

Lydia is a woman in her 70s who has been married to her husband for 55 years and has several adult children. She comes from a conservative Catholic background and has had a long history of difficulties with debilitating panic, agoraphobia, and depression. Additionally, she struggles with chronic guilt about many things that contribute to her psychological, behavioral, and relationship problems.

Jake is a middle-aged financial planner who is married and has several young daughters. He struggles with a pornography addiction and feels that it is out of control. Since he has become a parent, he has become especially troubled by his addiction. Furthermore, he considers himself a deeply moral, ethical, and religious man as well. His pornography problems contradict his more idealized view of himself. His wife caught him engaging with pornography, resulting in a marital crisis.

Adam is a 16-year-old teenager experiencing autism. He has become highly religious and adamant about engaging in multiple religious rituals that occupy much of his day. His parents and family are not very religious. They are very worried about the obsessive nature of Adam's religious behaviors and elaborate rituals. His grades are slipping, and he feels more and more isolated from his peers at school as well.

Spirituality (and Religion) Can Be Potentially Healthy or Unhealthy

Lydia, Jake, and Adam struggle with challenging issues that many other people experience. They may or may not be fully engaged by spiritual and religious matters and traditions, but they are influenced by them and might benefit from them as well. Religion and spirituality can certainly be a double-edged sword in that they can be employed in a healthy and productive manner or used in an unhealthy and destructive manner. So often people have a binary view of religion and spirituality, believing that they can be either all good or all bad. Yet, like most things in life, faith is more complicated than it may appear at first glance. Religion and spirituality can be used for great good or for great harm (Pargament, 2002; Whitehouse, 2019). Those who happen to be engaged by religion and spirituality tend to see the good outweighing the harm, while those who are not engaged with religion and spirituality tend to focus on the harm rather than the good.

1

There is a large body of quality empirical research that has examined both the productive and destructive nature of religion and spirituality (e.g., AbdAleati et al., 2016; Mochon et al., 2011; Plante, 2009; Vardy, 2014). Religious and spiritual engagement has been found to be associated with better physical and mental health as well as better social relationships (e.g., Plante & Sherman, 2001; Weber & Pargament, 2014). Yet religion and spirituality can be destructive, exclusionary, and contribute to in- versus out-group conflicts as well as violence (e.g., Iannaccone et al., 2006).

Perhaps an analogy regarding the helpful and destructive nature of fire can help us better understand and appreciate the risks and benefits of religious and spiritual engagement and influence. We all know that fire can be helpful to assist in cooking and keeping us warm. Many of our modern conveniences like stoves and heaters depend on fire. Survival would be difficult, if not impossible, if we did not learn how to use and manage it. Yet fire can also be extremely destructive when out of control and it can easily destroy homes and lives, and it can total vast natural environments when it spreads in an unchecked and destructive manner. Arsonists use fire to harm others, while chefs use fire to feed the multitudes. So, is fire good or bad? It depends on how it is used. The same is true with religion and spirituality. Like fire, it can be life giving and helpful for survival. Yet in the wrong hands or used in the wrong way, it can be destructive, leading to violence and other serious personal and societal problems. Fire and religion have much in common and can be used for good or for bad.

Why This Book?

This book hopes to provide you with a fuller understanding and appreciation of how spiritual and religious traditions and strategies can be helpful and impactful in your day-to-day life. The book will demonstrate how many of the strategies, principles, techniques, and perspectives finely tuned and refined by these often-ancient traditions can be used as intended or even secularized to benefit people live their best lives. Religious and spiritual tools and perspectives can be successfully utilized with people who have no spiritual or religious connections, affiliations, or interests at all. We all could use helpful tools that might improve our lives and better cope with an increasingly challenging world (Weber & Pargament, 2014). This book hopes to introduce and demonstrate how many of these tools can be effectively used to enhance the lives of people from diverse backgrounds and life experiences. Imagine discovering a large chest full of helpful tools located in an attic or basement that has been there all along but not opened or appreciated by those passing by. This book hopes to dust off and open this chest full of tools and demonstrate how many of these ancient ideas, perspectives, traditions, and strategies can be used in our complex contemporary lives.

So Many People Experience Mental Health, Behavioral, and Relationship Challenges

People are really struggling. The incidence of behavioral health problems and psychiatric challenges are exploding in what many have been calling a mental health tsunami (American Psychological Association, 2022; Canady, 2021; Office of the Surgeon General, 2021). The incidence of anxiety, depression, and substance abuse disorders is on the rise as well as suicidality and other serious mental health and behavioral problems (Duong et al., 2021). The U.S. surgeon general issued an unprecedented advisory at the end of 2021 highlighting the current mental health crisis and underscored that youth are especially impacted (Office of the Surgeon General, 2021). The number of people seeking mental health services has also exploded, and hospitals, clinics, schools, and university counseling centers have been scrambling to hire more mental health professionals while trying to find the funds to support these new hires and the important and critically needed services that they provide (Saunders et al., 2021).

Numerous factors contribute to the rise in mental health difficulties that include a blend of biological, psychological, social, and cultural influences. Many people are struggling to cope with increasingly difficult times in society. Rapidly increasing challenges with climate change, increasing economic instability and disparity, increasing polarization and divisive politics, the global COVID-19 pandemic, racism and discrimination, increasing incivility in our social and online relationships, the negative impact of social media, and many additional factors create chronic stress leading to psychological distress and psychiatric disorders (e.g., Listernick & Badawy, 2021). Additionally, social media has created an online environment where extreme upward social comparisons contribute to anxiety, depression, and low self-esteem among many users, most especially youth (Mueller, 2021). Unrealistically high expectations for happiness and success are all around us, fueled by narratives from movies, social media, wellness gurus, YouTube and TikTok influencers, and others.

The Religious and Spiritual Traditions Add to Our Life Skills Toolbox

In recent decades, some of the wisdom, strategies, and techniques used for centuries within religious and spiritual communities and traditions have been secularized to use by anyone who might experience a wide range of psychological, behavioral, and relationship stressors. Mindfulness-Based Stress Reduction (MBSR) is perhaps the best example of this trend (e.g., Arthington, 2016; Germer et al., 2013; Khoury et al., 2013). Mindfulness meditation comes from the Buddhist tradition, but it has been carefully secularized so that this approach appeals to people regardless of their religious or spiritual affiliations or interests (Shonin, 2015; Sun, 2014). One does not need to be a practicing Buddhist to use and benefit from mindfulness meditation strategies. Yoga is another excellent example of the secularization of a religious or spiritual tool or approach. While yoga comes from the Hindu tradition, it also has been carefully secularized in a way to appeal to people from all or no spiritual or religious traditions (e.g., Khalsa, 2013; Newcombe & O'Brien-Kop, 2020). One does not need to be a practicing Hindu to participate and benefit from yoga. Both mindfulness and yoga have become very popular among diverse populations across the globe. However, the versions practiced in North America, Europe, and elsewhere have little connection to the deep and extensive religious and spiritual traditions from where they originated (Germer et al., 2013; Plante, 2016). Additionally, many people seem to feel more comfortable with and accepting of spiritual traditions and strategies that come from nonproselytizing traditions such as Buddhism and Hinduism (Twenge et al., 2016; Uecker, 2007). Many people feel less comfortable or even threatened by spiritual techniques and strategies that originate from proselytizing traditions (e.g., Christianity, Islam). Therefore, people may be skeptical or reluctant to utilize spiritual approaches and techniques that they perceive as having a hidden agenda of conversion (Vardy, 2014).

It is unfortunate that many people can be rejecting of potentially helpful strategies for better living based upon religious and spiritual traditions that they either affiliate with or not. All the major religious and spiritual traditions offer centuries of wisdom and fine-tuning of strategies for more effective living and better coping with various life stressors (Pargament et al., 2013; Plante, 2009). We all can learn a great deal from these traditions that have developed many effective methods of managing life's troubles over so many years.

What Are Spiritually Informed Life Principles?

Spiritually informed life principles involve utilizing the wisdom of the spiritual and religious traditions from one or more perspectives to enhance our lives. They may include techniques, perspectives, strategies, and interventions of the spiritual and religious traditions and adapting them to use by anyone. They offer value-added tools to our coping and life management toolbox. They can be used in ways that are acceptable to both religious and nonreligious populations.

Highlighting Jesuit Influences in Spiritually Informed Life Principles

This book hopes to introduce you to religious and spiritual techniques that could be used regardless of one's spiritual or religious interests, affiliations, or traditions. In particular, I will highlight the contributions from the Jesuits. The Jesuits are a Roman Catholic religious order founded about 500 years ago by St. Ignatius of Loyola (Martin, 2013; Mottola, 1964; O'Malley, 1993). The Jesuits are well-known for being contemplatives in action, offering highly sought after spiritual direction, running high schools and universities, and engaging in social justice–related ministries across the globe (Barry & Doherty, 2014; Mottola, 1964). There are about 150 Jesuit colleges and universities in the world with 27 in the United States alone (e.g., Georgetown, Boston College, Santa Clara, and Loyola; Schwickerath, 2011). Jesuits work in such diverse fields as medicine, law, engineering, science, humanities, and psychology. The current pope, Pope Francis, is a Jesuit (Scannone, 2016).

Certainly, other religious orders within the Roman Catholic faith tradition (e.g., Franciscans, Dominicans) as well as other non-Catholic and non-Christian religious traditions offer much to the community, and this book will not focus exclusively on Jesuit contributions. Many books could be written on how contributions from various religious and spiritual traditions can be used to improve our lives (Plante, 2018). One book cannot do justice to all the contributions from these diverse perspectives, traditions, and communities. For the sake of this book, I will highlight Jesuit influences while addressing those of others periodically.

Why the Jesuits?

I have worked at a Jesuit university (Santa Clara University) for about 30 years and have been actively engaged and impressed with this religious tradition. In my role as a college professor and as a licensed psychologist in clinical practice for 35 years, I have had the opportunity to learn and incorporate numerous Jesuit influences and developed strategies and techniques for better living into my professional work (e.g., research, consultation, teaching, psychotherapy). I have used these approaches with my clinical patients, advised my university students with great success, and conducted empirical research including randomized controlled clinical trials on several of these Jesuit approaches and techniques. People from religious or nonreligious communities can use these approaches and, thus, be secularized in a similar way that mindfulness and yoga have done so successfully.

These Jesuit techniques and approaches are very popular within Jesuit circles. Those who are interested in and engaged by the *Spiritual Exercises of St. Ignatius* are familiar with them (Mottola, 1964). Those who have attended Jesuit high schools, colleges, universities, retreat centers, or other Jesuit-influenced institutions have likely learned and hopefully benefited from these approaches. However, those outside of this circle likely have never encountered them. Again, I am reminded of how mindfulness meditation approaches were well known within Buddhist environments while yoga was popular in India among Hindus. Outside of these circles, these helpful approaches were not readily available or used until more recent years. Thus, I hope to do with Jesuit strategies what has been successfully accomplished with mindfulness and yoga. Since most people are aware of the benefits of mindfulness and yoga, but not typically aware of Jesuit influences, this book will introduce them to these Jesuit-inspired approaches that have been hiding in full view for many years (Plante, 2020).

Seven Jesuit-Influenced Approaches

In this book, I will focus on the following seven Jesuit-influenced approaches or perspectives that can be well suited to better life skills. They include:

1. Seeing God (or the sacred) in all things
2. *Cura personalis* (i.e., care for the whole person)
3. The four *D*s of discernment and decision making
4. Using the Examen as an end-of-day review and reflection
5. Managing conflict with accommodation, humility, and the expectation of goodness
6. A path to kinship with civility, hospitality, solidarity, and mutuality
7. Ethical decision-making strategies

While I will briefly introduce each of these approaches here, the rest of the book will include full chapters on each one with a variety of examples and exercises so that you can integrate them into your life. Additionally, towards the end of the book, I will include many other, non-Jesuit–inspired, tools for spiritually informed life principles as well.

1. Seeing God (or the Sacred) in All Things

Seeing God (or the sacred) in all things means that if we truly experience others as being sacred, important, and possessing an element of the divine within them, then we will experience and treat people respectfully and with great care and compassion. Too often in our contemporary society we see others with whom we disagree or do not like as being less than sacred and, tragically, often less than human. We can too easily demonize our enemies or those who are not in our tribe or community. Tribal tendencies are common and have been so perhaps since humans first roamed the earth. Tribal identities are often based on race, ethnicity, gender, social class, country of origin, proximity, political persuasions, religion, schools attended, and even among sport spectators. Seeing God (or the sacred) in all is a strong foil against tribalism in that it underscores the notion that we are all connected as brothers and sisters, and all have the sacred or divine within us (Wilson, 2021).

2. *Cura Personalis* (i.e., Care for the Whole Person)

Cura personalis is an important and core concept and approach within Jesuit spirituality and perspective (Mottola, 1964). It means caring and attending to the whole person. *Cura personalis* has enormous implications in terms of how we interact with others and think about ourselves as well. *Cura personalis* is consistent with the popular and contemporary biopsychosocial model (Engel, 1977; Melchert, 2011) of attending to the biological, psychological, and social needs of people and that these various elements of human experience all interact with each other. Thus, *cura personalis* is a constant reminder that people do not behave or struggle in a vacuum but rather have multiple elements and influences in their lives that they must manage and contend with and that the whole person needs to be attended to.

3. The Four *D*s of Discernment and Decision Making

The four *D*s of discernment are a helpful structure and pathway for making life decisions. Certainly, we all need to be good about making important life decisions and the four *D*s can help us all to do so. They include the process of discovery of one's gifts, talents, and desires followed by a period of detachment from the influence of other voices that often may not be positive influences in our lives. These voices could include those expressed by family, friends, colleagues, society in general, and many other influences. The third step in the decision-making process is discernment with ongoing reflection about what provides us with consolation versus desolation. Finally, we find direction through this ongoing process of discernment. The four *D*s can be utilized in making both small and large decisions and can be used in an ongoing way to update and fine tune one's direction and decisions over time (Plante, 2017).

4. Using the Examen as an End-of-Day Review and Reflection

The Examen is an end of day reflection and process that includes five steps completed within about 15 minutes (Manney, 2011; McMillin, 2021). The first step of the Examen is to put oneself in God's (or the sacred as understood by the participant) presence. The second step encourages one to give thanks and be grateful for various points and experiences, both big and small, in one's day. The third step reviews the experiences of the current day reflecting on what went well and not so well while focusing on the presence of the divine or sacred during key moments and inflection points during the day. The fourth step encourages a reflection on one's shortcomings where improvement in thought and behavior might be needed or desired moving forward. The final step includes planning and looking forward to the next day while reflecting upon and learning from the review of the current day. The Examen can be completed in a religious, spiritual, or secularized manner (Plante, 2021).

5. Managing Conflict with Accommodation, Humility, and the Expectation of Goodness

Managing conflict with accommodation, humility, and the expectation of goodness is an important three-step strategy for negotiating the challenges of interpersonal and intergroup conflicts so prevalent today (Exercices Spirituels de Discernement Apostolique en Commun, 2016). Accommodation refers to trying to understand the views of another. It does not mean that you agree with the other person or group but rather that you try to enter their world to understand their perspective and viewpoints. It asks: Can you see the world or various issues through the lens of another, even if you disagree with them? Humility means approaching others with whom you disagree, humbly accepting that no one has a corner on the truth and that we all could learn from the perspectives of others, even when we feel strongly about something. Humility is a foil to arrogance and narcissism. It suggests that we have something to learn from others, even when we feel that we are in the right and they are clearly in the wrong. Finally, the expectation of goodness refers to the default option that we should maintain that others are trying to do what is right and good and that their intentions, even if misguided, are based in goodness or at least a desire for a good outcome from their point of view. The expectation of goodness asks: Can you give people the benefit of the doubt by assuming they are trying to do what is good and right even if it might be difficult for us to see it?

6. A Path to Kinship with Civility, Hospitality, Solidarity, and Mutuality

A charism or spirit of civility and hospitality refers to being kind, generous, and welcoming of others. Can we interact with others with a gracious and generous spirit? The Jewish bible, often referred to as the Old Testament or Tenak, offers a well-known story of strangers visiting Abraham's tent where Abraham treats them with great hospitality (Hartog, 2020). In the story, Abraham did not realize that his visitors were angels sent by God. Within the Christian tradition, one of the Rules of St. Benedict is to treat everyone, even the stranger, as if they are Jesus himself (Frey, 2018; Henry, 2021). These stories and perspectives provide a model or template for treating others with graciousness, generosity, and a hospitable spirit.

If we see God (or the sacred) in all things, then we can better appreciate the importance of everyone and the need to be connected and compassionate to all. Thus, pain experienced by others is, or should be, a concern for all of us. If everyone is a brother or sister connected by sacredness, then we must be in solidarity with one another as we face our various challenges in living. Being in solidarity suggests more than caring about the plight of others in distress or crisis; it also means that we all are invested in each other's well-being and must work together for the benefit of everyone. Solidarity underscores the common good and suggests that we are all in this world and life together. Solidarity implies mutuality and highlights kinship in that we all must experience each other as brothers and sisters within a large extended family (Plante, 2019).

Solidarity means that we put ourselves in the story of others by placing ourselves into the shoes of another to better understand and appreciate their perspective and see the world from the eyes of another. In religious communities, this might include putting oneself into biblical stories or narratives to help someone understand and appreciate various sides of challenging issues (Mottola, 1964). This technique is easily adapted to a general life principle to put ourselves into the shoes or narratives of others and learning from this perspective (Mann, 2010).

7. Ethical Decision-Making Strategies

All the religious and spiritual traditions offer thoughtful advice and wisdom about ethical strategies for living. Certainly, the Jesuits are not unique in this area, but they do highlight ethical strategies that may be especially helpful for managing our lives. Moral philosophy and religious ethics can be secularized in various ways to provide people with an active moral theory to handle challenges in living (Plante, 2004; Vaughn, 2015).

Additional Spirituality Informed Therapy Techniques and Principles

In addition to these nine strategies or principles that are borrowed from Jesuit spirituality and approaches to living, many other more general spiritually based tools can be incorporated into the psychotherapeutic process benefiting clients. I highlighted these tools in an earlier book for mental health professionals (Plante, 2009), but some are repeated here and will be integrated in this book as well. These include:

1. Prayer and Meditation

All the spiritual and religious traditions offer strategies for prayer and meditation (Eifring, 2013; Martin, 2021). Prayer comes in many forms and involves interaction or communication with the unseen (e.g., the divine and sacred) while meditation techniques also come in many forms and include strategies to quiet the mind, push away the many distractions of life, focus attention on an object or concept, and secure insight for better living. Some meditative approaches have been readily accepted in the general population (e.g., mindfulness), while many others have been ignored. A wide variety of meditative approaches and techniques can be added to one's life principles and coping toolbox.

2. Meaning, Purpose, and Calling

All the spiritual and religious traditions have something to say about meaning and purpose in life. They offer wisdom about how one should live one's life and provide direction to guide people in life decisions. Many of us are looking for meaning and purpose, and spiritual and religious traditions offer much in this regard.

3. Bibliotherapy

The spiritual and religious traditions offer a great deal when it comes to things to read. In addition to sacred scripture and commentary about scripture, the spiritual and religious traditions offer numerous applied readings on just about every aspect of human thought and behavior. These readings can be helpful to us.

4. Rituals and Community Events

All the spiritual and religious traditions offer rituals and community events for their members. These events can be especially helpful for people during life transitions such as births, coming of age, marriage, deaths, sickness, and transitioning from one stage of life to another.

5. Volunteerism

The religious and spiritual traditions offer charitable activities and opportunities for volunteerism. They host soup kitchens, low or no fee hospitals and clinics, food pantries, orphanages, relief services, migrant and refugee services and advocacy, and many others. Often we look to volunteer activities to find purpose and meaning, combat loneliness, or develop a supportive community. The religious and spiritual traditions tend to offer many opportunities across the globe for volunteer experiences that can be helpful to those looking for more meaning and purpose in their lives.

6. Social Justice

The religious and spiritual traditions have much to say about social justice and attending to the needs and concerns of the marginalized and voiceless in society. They offer advocacy services as well as support for those who are often poor or unable to advocate for themselves. Social justice activities can be appealing to many who may wish to volunteer with these endeavors or perhaps help those who have similar struggles in life.

7. Spiritual Models

The religious and spiritual traditions offer models for how to think and act. These models may be very well known like Jesus, Mohammad, Buddha, and various saints (e.g., Mother Teresa, Dorothy Day, Saint Francis of Assisi) or they may be local leaders or spiritual and religious exemplars (Oman et al., 2012). Decades of research on observational learning and social comparisons instructs us that we learn ways of thinking and behavior by watching important models (e.g., Bandura et al., 1966). The spiritual and religious traditions offer many high status exemplars from which to model our own thinking and behavior.

8. Being Part of Something Bigger Than Oneself

The spiritual and religious traditions offer a way to become part of something bigger and grander than oneself. They connect people to traditions, rituals, and communities that have been formed over centuries. Being part of something larger than ourselves or our own needs and lives can be helpful to many.

Conclusion

As we can see, there are numerous tools from the spiritual and religious traditions that can be incorporated into our life principles and coping skills. Some of these tools can be more easily secularized than others and so we need to be transparent about where these tools come from and how they might be used. The use and potential endorsement of these spiritual and religious tools are not efforts to proselytize or evangelize. The remaining part of this book will unpack and explicate these tools so that the reader can have a better appreciation and start developing the skills to use them. Many examples and exercises will be offered as well.

Further Reading

James, W. (1936). *The varieties of religious experience: A study in human nature.* Modern Library. (Original work published 1902).

Martin, M. (2013). *The Jesuits.* Simon and Schuster.

Mottola, A. (1964). *The Spiritual exercises of St. Ignatius: St. Ignatius' profound precepts of mystical theology.* Doubleday.

Plante, T. G. (2009). *Spiritual practices in psychotherapy: Thirteen tools for enhancing psychological health.* American Psychological Association.

Plante, T. G. (Ed.). (2018). *Healing with spiritual practices: Proven techniques for disorders from addictions and anxiety to cancer and chronic pain.* Praeger/ABC-CLIO.

Plante, T. G. (2020). St. Ignatius as psychotherapist? How Jesuit spirituality and wisdom can enhance psychotherapy. *Spirituality in Clinical Practice, 7*(1) 65–71.

References

AbdAleati, N. S., Zaharim, N. M., & Mydin, Y. O. (2016). Religiousness and mental health: Systematic review study. *Journal of Religion and Health, 55*(6), 1929–1937.

American Psychological Association. (2022). APA Stress in America survey. Author.

Arthington, P. (2016). Mindfulness: A critical perspective. *Community Psychology in Global Perspective, 2*(1), 87–104.

Bandura, A., Grusec, J. E., & Menlove, F. L. (1966). Observational learning as a function of symbolization and incentive set. *Child development, 37*(3), 499–506. https://doi.org/10.2307/1126674

Barry, W. A., & Doherty, R. G. (2014). *Contemplatives in action: The Jesuit way.* Paulist Press.

Canady, V. A. (2021). APA survey: Majority of Americans reporting prolonged stress. *Mental Health Weekly, 31*(6), 6.

Duong, M. T., Bruns, E. J., Lee, K., Cox, S., Coifman, J., Mayworm, A., & Lyon, A. R. (2021). Rates of mental health service utilization by children and adolescents in schools and other common service settings: A systematic review and meta-analysis. *Administration and Policy in Mental Health and Mental Health Services Research, 48*(3), 420–439. DOI: 10.1007/s10488-020-01080-9

Eifring, H. (2013). Meditation in Judaism, Christianity and Islam: Technical aspects of devotional practices. In *Meditation in Judaism, Christianity and Islam: Cultural histories,* 1–13.

Engel, G. L. (1977). The need for a new medical model: A challenge for biomedicine. *Science, 196*(4286), 129–136.

Exercices Spirituels de Discernement Apostolique en Commun (ESDAC) (2016). *Welcoming and building communion together: Manual for facilitators.* Author.

Frey, S. M. (2018). Humility rules: Saint Benedict's twelve-step guide to genuine self-esteem. *The Catholic Library World, 88*(3), 215.

Germer, C. K., Siegel, R. D, & Fulton, P. R. (Eds.). (2013). *Mindfulness and psychotherapy* (2nd ed.). Guilford Press.

Hartog, P. (2020). Abraham and the rhetoric of hospitality and foreignness in Hebrews and 1 Clement. *Science et Esprit, 72*(3), 281–296.

Henry, P. (2021). *Benedictine Options: Learning to Live from the Sons and Daughters of Saints Benedict and Scholastica.* Liturgical Press.

Iannaccone, L. R., & Berman, E. (2006). Religious extremism: The good, the bad, and the deadly. *Public Choice, 128*(1/2), 109–129.

Khalsa, S. B. S. (2013). Yoga for psychiatry and mental health: An ancient practice with modern relevance. *Indian Journal of Psychiatry, 55*(Suppl 3), S334.

Khoury, B., Lecomte, T., Fortin, G., Masse, M., Therien, P., Bouchard, V., Chapleau, M.-A., Paquin, K., & Hofmann, S. G. (2013). Mindfulness-based therapy: A comprehensive meta-analysis. *Clinical Psychology Review, 33*(6), 763–771.

Listernick, Z. I., & Badawy, S. M. (2021). Mental health implications of the COVID-19 pandemic among children and adolescents: What do we know so far? *Pediatric Health, Medicine and Therapeutics, 12,* 543–549. doi: 10.2147/PHMT.S315887

Mann, D. (2010). *Gestalt therapy: 100 key points & techniques.* Routledge.

Manney, J. (2011). *A simple, life-changing prayer: Discovering the power of St. Ignatius Loyola's Examen*. Loyola Press.

Martin, J. (2021). *Learning to pray: A guide for everyone*. HarperOne.

McMillin, S. E. (2021). Innovating vocational resilience: Getting a second start at work through the Ignatian Examen. *Social Work & Christianity, 48*(1), 5–9.

Melchert, T. P. (2011). *Foundations of professional psychology: The end of theoretical orientations and the emergence of the biopsychosocial approach*. Elsevier.

Mochon, D., Norton, M. I., & Ariely, D. (2011). Who benefits from religion? *Social Indicators Research, 101*(1), 1–15.

Mottola, A. (1964). *The Spiritual Exercises of St. Ignatius: St. Ignatius' profound precepts of mystical theology*. Doubleday.

Mueller, T. S. (2021). Blame, then shame? Psychological predictors in cancel culture behavior. *Social Science Journal*, 1–14. https://doi.org/10.1080/03623319.2021.1949552

Newcombe, S., & O'Brien-Kop, K. (Eds.). (2020). *Routledge handbook of yoga and meditation studies*. Routledge.

Office of the Surgeon General. (2021). *Protecting youth mental health: The U.S. Surgeon General's advisory*. Author.

O'Malley, J. W. (1993). *The first Jesuits*. Harvard University Press.

Oman, D., Thoresen, C. E., Park, C. L., Shaver, P. R., Hood, R. W., & Plante, T. G. (2012). Spiritual modeling self-efficacy. *Psychology of Religion and Spirituality, 4*(4), 278–297. https://doi.org/10.1037/a0027941

Pargament, K. I. (2002). The bitter and the sweet: An evaluation of the costs and benefits of religiousness. *Psychological Inquiry, 13*(3), 168–181.

Pargament, K. I., Exline, J., Jones, J. W., & Shafranske, E. P. (2013). *APA handbook of psychology, religion, and spirituality*. American Psychological Association.

Plante, T. G. (2004). *Do the right thing: Living ethically in an unethical world*. New Harbinger.

Plante, T. G. (2009). *Spiritual Practices in Psychotherapy: Thirteen Tools for Enhancing Psychological Health*. American Psychological Association.

Plante, T. G. (2016). Beyond mindfulness: Expanding integration of spirituality and religion into psychotherapy. *Open Theology, 2*(1), 135–144.

Plante, T. G. (2017). The 4 Ds: Using Ignatian spirituality in secular psychotherapy and beyond. *Spirituality in Clinical Practice, 4*(1), 74–79. https://doi.org/10.1037/scp0000122

Plante, T. G. (Ed.). (2018). *Healing with spiritual practices: Proven techniques for disorders from addictions and anxiety to cancer and chronic pain*. Praeger/ABC-CLIO.

Plante, T. G. (2019). Possible next steps in APA's civility efforts: Moving from civility to hospitality, solidarity, and to kinship. *The Specialist, 44*, 23–26.

Plante, T. G. (2020). St. Ignatius as psychotherapist? How Jesuit spirituality and wisdom can enhance psychotherapy. *Spirituality in Clinical Practice, 7*(1), 65–71. https://doi.org/10.1037/scp0000214

Plante, T. G. (2021). Using the Examen, a Jesuit prayer, in spiritually integrated and secular psychotherapy, *Pastoral Psychology. 71*, 119–125. DOI:10.1007/s11089-021-00967-0

Plante, T. G., & Sherman, A. C. (Eds.) (2001). *Faith and health: Psychological perspectives*. Guilford.

Saunders, R., Buckman, J. E. J., Fonagy, P., & Fancourt, D. (2021). Understanding different trajectories of mental health across the general population during the COVID-19 pandemic. *Psychological medicine*, 1–9. DOI: 10.1017/S0033291721000957

Scannone, J. C. (2016). Pope Francis and the theology of the people. *Theological Studies, 77*(1), 118–135.

Schwickerath, R. (2011). *Jesuit education: Its history and principles viewed in the light of modern educational problems*. Read Books Ltd.

Shonin, E., Van Gordon, W., & Singh, N. N. (Eds.). (2015). *Buddhist foundations of mindfulness*. Springer.

Sun, J. (2014). Mindfulness in context: A historical discourse analysis. *Contemporary Buddhism, 15*(2), 394–415.

Twenge, J. M., Sherman, R. A., Exline, J. J., & Grubbs, J. B. (2016). Declines in American adults' religious participation and beliefs, 1972–2014. *Sage Open, 6*(1), 2158244016638133.

Uecker, J. E., Regnerus, M. D., & Vaaler, M. L. (2007). Losing my religion: The social sources of religious decline in early adulthood. *Social Forces, 85*(4), 1667–1692.

Vardy, P. (2014). *Good and Bad Religion*. SCM Press.

Vaughn, L. (2015). *Beginning ethics: An introduction to moral philosophy*. Norton.

Weber, S. R., & Pargament, K. I. (2014). The role of religion and spirituality in mental health. *Current Opinion in Psychiatry, 27*(5), 358–363.

Whitehouse, H. (2019). Has religion been good or bad for humanity? Epic analysis delivers an answer. *New Scientist, 242*(3224), 36–39.

Wilson, A. (2021). *God of all things: Rediscovering the sacred in an everyday world*. Zondervan.

CHAPTER 2

Seeing God (or the Sacred) in All Things

An important principle and perspective in Jesuit spirituality is seeing or finding God (or the sacred) in all things (Carls, 2017; Healey, 2014; Hellwig, 1994). Of course, this notion of sacredness and the divine being everywhere and in all of creation is not unique to the Jesuits and is highlighted and found among many other diverse spiritualties and religious traditions (Taylor, 2017). For example, you may be familiar with the greeting "Namaste," often used by Hindus and those who live in India and other parts of the world. It is a greeting that is typically offered with clasped hands and a slight bow when meeting others, including strangers, colleagues, family members, and friends alike. The word *Namaste* comes from Sanskrit and is usually interpreted as meaning that the divine and sacred in me recognizes the divine and sacred in you (Sharma et al., 2021). It is a beautiful and inspiring sentiment that underscores how everyone is important, special, worthy, and sacred (Oxhandler, 2017). Of course, some people might simply interpret a Namaste greeting as just saying, "Hello," but the notion of recognizing and acknowledging the divine and sacred in others offers a perspective on life and attitude towards others that is very important to embrace and can be helpfully integrated into general life principles (Corbett, 2011; Pargament, 2011; Sandage & Strawn, 2022).

Nurturing the view that the divine lives within others, however personally interpreted and understood, and ourselves is a transformative way to see and exist in the world (Taylor, 2017). Using terms like *God, Jesus, Allah, Adonai, the Great Spirit, higher power*, or even *love, humanity, peace*, or another meaningful word or phrase, can evoke the "divine" concept in their own way. It is like putting on a new set of tinted or colored glasses so that the world is now viewed in a unique and special way that changes your perspective and reactions. Everything and everybody become more important, special, valued, and sacred. If you fully embrace this perspective and way of viewing others, then you will find yourself thinking about and behaving towards others in different and likely much more positive ways (e.g., Pargament, 2011; Simard & Volicer, 2010).

Before providing some examples, exercises, and applications of this approach to life, let us define *sacred*. *Sacred* tends to refer to what is highly valued and worthy of attention and reverence (Engler & Gardiner, 2017). While it is often used to refer to religious ideas, deities, and something holy, it can be used in more general and global ways to refer to important concepts or qualities that are not secular or profane. Regardless of one's religious or spiritual tradition, affiliation, or interests, the sacred refers to something very important and valued (Emmons, 2005).

So, how does finding God (and the sacred) in all things assist in developing principles for better living (Griffith & Griffith, 2003)? Frequently, people experience conflicts, tensions, and various difficulties in their relationships with others and even with themselves. They may experience marital or relationship distress, conflicts with their children, relatives, neighbors, coworkers, and many others. They may also struggle with their relationship with themselves by maintaining a low self-esteem, debilitating guilt, or feeling unworthy of love and attention. They may have such a challenged view of themselves that they consider or attempt suicide or engage in other self-destructive thoughts and behaviors. They also may experience narcissistic defenses, thinking or behaving in a way that suggests that no one is good enough for them and that others are simply inferior and not worthy of their love, attention, time, or respect. If people can see God (or the sacred) in *all* things, including both themselves as well as others, then this perspective can help them treat both themselves and others with more dignity, respect, compassion, and value. It elevates how they view themselves and others in ways that can be parlayed into better relationships and perspectives (Corbett, 2011; Pargament, 2011; Simard & Volicer, 2010).

Perhaps several examples can be helpful to demonstrate how seeing or finding God (or the sacred) in all things can be worthwhile to consider.

Case Example 2.1 Jake

Jake, the married middle-aged man with several young daughters, was introduced in the first chapter. He struggles with pornography addiction, is troubled by his pornography consumption since he is a family man, and prides himself on being a moral, ethical, and religiously engaged person. A few more details about Jake and his pornography addiction might be helpful to see how the notion that God (or the sacred) being in all things can help him better manage his troubling addictive behavior. Like many young men in our contemporary culture, Jake used pornography when he was a teenager during his developmentally appropriate and expected sexual awakening. He was curious and interested in sexuality and began noticing and being attracted to appealing girls in his school about the time he was going through puberty during his late middle school years. These new feelings resulted in engaging in masturbation as well as viewing easily accessible pornography through various internet websites. Some of his friends admitted to pornography use as well and shared websites that they found especially appealing. Jake associated pornography with sexual arousal and satisfaction. In terms of conditioning, Jake conditioned himself in a way that pornography was associated with sexual release and expression.

Jake met his now wife, Julie, while they were in college. Jake and Julie shared many similar interests, and Jake found her to be pretty and friendly. He described himself as a "perfect gentleman" while they dated. However, once they became sexually intimate, he found that sexual engagement with Julie was "okay but kind of boring." While he generally enjoyed sexual intimacy with Julie, he found his pornography use accompanied by masturbation to be much more exciting and rewarding. He had learned to associate the high degree of stimulation with pornography with deeper sexual satisfaction. Sexual activity with Julie just did not seem very interesting or as exciting to Jake. Julie could sense that his sexual engagement with her was rather uninspired, and when she caught Jake using pornography, she was emotionally hurt and concluded that Jake was not sexually attracted to her. She could tell that their sexual life was less satisfying than pornography use for Jake. Julie felt rejected and angry, too. She expressed that she felt inadequate since who could compete with the excitement of pornography and such beautiful and sexy actors.

Jake responded to Julie with some degree of defensiveness saying that pornography use was "really no big deal" and that it did not reflect on their marital relationship at all. However, Jake admitted that he felt guilty about it and felt sorry to have upset Julie. He also thought that one day his daughters might catch him in the act of using pornography and that if they did, he (and they) might be completely devastated.

Jake was committed to change his behavior but found it challenging since he had used pornography for many years and besides feeling a bit guilty, he really enjoyed it. The notion of finding God (and the sacred) in all things was introduced to Jake to help him better manage the appeal of pornography.

Jake was encouraged to consider that the particular sexy women he was looking at on the pornography websites were real people, not just objects for his sexual satisfaction. He was encouraged to reflect on who these women were and what kind of lives and family situations they came from. He was encouraged to develop narratives about them, giving them real names and stories about their families, interests, and desires for productive work outside of the pornography industry. Jake was encouraged to read or listen to real stories about sex workers and the lives that they lead off camera. Jake was encouraged to watch a television special produced by CNN that interviewed sex workers to better understand their lives and the circumstances that lead to working in the pornography industry. He learned that many of these women had challenging lives, children to care for, and could not resist the much-needed money that the pornography industry offered. He learned that many were uncomfortable and embarrassed by their work and felt too guilty to reveal this to most of their friends and relatives. Throughout this process, Jake was encouraged to remind himself that each of these pornography actors were sacred, children of God, and important. They were real people with real stories and likely felt compelled to work in the pornography industry because they felt that they had little choice in the matter due to various life circumstances and difficulties. They would have preferred a different lifestyle and career path. They were not sexual toys or objects for his and other's gratification but really people and sacred people too.

As Jake worked on this new perception of pornography actors, their sexual appeal became less tantalizing. He had a harder time objectifying them as mere sex objects. He began to experience them and think of them as brothers and sisters. This notion of seeing the sacred and divine within these actors made their sexual appeal less compelling.

Case Example 2.2 Lydia

Lydia was also introduced in the first chapter. She has a long history of agoraphobia, panic disorder, and depression. Lydia is also problematically judgmental towards certain others. For example, she decided that she hated her son's fiancée, Allie. She felt that Allie was snobby, bossy, and "too good" for the "little people," like her family. Lydia vowed to not attend the upcoming wedding. Her stance upset her husband and other family members, and her son was worried that she would follow through with her threat.

Actually, Lydia felt intimidated by Allie and her more successful and highly educated family. They all had advanced degrees, were much wealthier than Lydia's family, and belonged to an expensive country club and traveled extensively. Lydia felt inferior and awkward being around Allie and her family. Lydia and her husband never attended college and Lydia was a stay-at-home mother while her husband worked at a blue-collar job. They lived in a modest home and never traveled beyond short driving trips. Lydia could appreciate that her self-esteem challenges contributed to her views of Allie and her family.

Lydia was receptive to embracing the notion that God and the sacred are in all things and to try to see the sacred in Allie and her family. Lydia was also encouraged to see the sacred and divine in herself as well, even if she had less education, money, and sophistication than Allie and her family. Lydia worked to see the positive qualities in Allie and her family and more positive qualities in herself as well.

Lydia attended the wedding but admitted that she took a Xanax beforehand to calm her nerves. She reported that she had a ball at the wedding and danced more than just about anyone else at the wedding reception did. She expressed gratitude that she attended and proudly concluded that she was a better dancer than Allie's mother was.

Case Example 2.3 Adam

Adam was also introduced in the first chapter. He is a teenager who struggles with autism and religious scrupulosity (i.e., pathological guilt and anxiety about religious and moral issues and behavior that can be obsessive and compulsive). Religious rituals that take much of his time and energy burden him. His parents are worried and even mortified about how seriously he takes these religious beliefs and practices. Adam was very open to the notion of finding God (and the sacred) in all things as it is consistent with his religious beliefs and practices. However, since Adam is religiously highly conservative, he can be judgmental and dismissive of nonconservative approaches to spirituality and religion. While he was open to the perspective of finding God and the sacred in all things, he was hesitant when he learned that this perspective is closely associated with Jesuit spirituality and traditions. He was leery of Jesuit influences since he and many others consider the Jesuits as being very progressive and representing the more liberal wing of the Catholic Church.

Over time, Adam grew to understand that parts of his rituals were associated with his guilt about masturbation as well as angry impulses that he experiences towards those whom he does not like or get along with, including some peers at school. Since he experiences autism, he has some troubles in social relationships and periodically fellow students will criticize and demean him. Occasionally, he is bullied. Since he tends to indulge in black-or-white thinking, he easily concludes that people are either good or bad, saints or sinners. Using the notion of seeing God or the sacred in all things, Adam comes to realize that he needs to work on having a more accepting and embracing approach to others and even to those with whom he does not agree or like. Additionally, he works on developing a more accepting view of himself and experiencing himself as being sacred, even with his faults and shortcomings. He is introduced to the popular quote from sacred scripture, "All have sinned and fallen short of the glory of God" (Romans 3:23) that he uses as a mantra to remind himself that he and others all are far from perfect but that we all are sacred and children of God nonetheless. As Adam becomes more accepting of himself and others and open to the feedback and influences of others of good will, even if they are not as conservative as he is, his rituals are lessened, and he has more time and energy for school, family, and other appropriate teenage activities and concerns.

In these diverse examples that involve people with very different types of concerns, life difficulties, and resources, the notion of seeing God (and the sacred) in all things is an important notion for process in coping. It is a perspective and a way of looking at the world and the people in it with more reverence, dignity, and gentleness. It acts as a foil to being judgmental and rejecting and condemning both self and others. It can help with self-esteem issues as well as conflicts with people and groups.

Five Strategies for Nurturing and Finding God (or the Sacred) in All Things

How can we nurture and promote a perspective in which we're finding God (or the sacred) in all things? What general principles, strategies, techniques, and prompts can help us all embrace this important way of seeing the world and the people in it? There are several strategies that might help us to more fully embrace and live within this perspective.

1. Recognize What You Already Find Sacred and Expand Upon It

Most people have some sense of what is critically important and even sacred to them. They may or may not articulate these experiences or interests as being divine or use the word *sacred* when describing them (Engler & Gardiner, 2017). These might include being in nature or in a relationship with someone special, such as a spouse, child, parent, or dear friend. It could also include enjoying a special place or a special meal. Most people can identify a number of people, places, or experiences where they experience something very important, holy, and sacred regardless of the actual words that they use to describe their experience or relationship. We can nurture these insights by putting helpful words to them and encouraging clients to deepen and widen their appreciation for them. We can investigate why they hold these places, people, experiences, and moments as sacred and more fully understand how they can be transformative for the client. We can examine if there might be ways to expand these experiences and perspectives to find sacredness elsewhere and ultimately in all things.

Exercise 2.1 What Is Sacred to You?

What is sacred to you? Reflect on the most important people, places, and values that you hold need and dear. List them out. Try to list 10 items on your sacred list. Can you also rank them from most sacred to least? What does this list, once completed, tell you about yourself and your life priorities? Jot those down too. What does this exercise tell you about yourself and your life principles and goals?

Top 10 most sacred people, places, and values in your life (in rank order)

1. _____

2. _____

3. _____

4. _____

5. _____

6. _____

7. _____

8. _____

9. _____

10. _____

What does this list say about your priorities in life?

_____

_____

What does this exercise tell you about yourself and your life principles and goals?

_____

_____

_____

2. Embrace the Wonder and Complexity of Life

The more we learn about life in all forms and at all levels, the more we recognize how remarkably complex it all seems to be. Of course, we expect humans and large animals to be complex, but the bodies and lives of insects, fish, and even very basic life forms (e.g., jellyfish, yeast) are so much more intricate and complicated than they appear at first glance. Various books and documentary films have highlighted this notion and can help us to develop a sense of the sacred in more places and among all things. For example, a popular documentary film (*My Octopus Teacher*) about the life of an octopus and its amazingly intimate relationship with the human filmmaker became a sensation and underscored the complexity and relational features of these complex creatures (Ross, 2021; Thys, 2020). Many people found the film riveting and admitted that they can never see an octopus in the same light again. Many also felt that they could not eat them again either (Jones et al., 2021). Famous scholars such as E. O. Wilson have studied the intricate lives and behaviors of insects such as ants (Hölldobler & Wilson, 1990; Wilson, 1963, 1988). The complexity of their lives is remarkable and amazing to learn about. One cannot experience ants in the same way after learning about their complex lives and communities. While they can be an annoying nuisance when they occasionally take over kitchen counters, even these pests can be viewed in a sacred way after learning about them in more detail.

Exercise 2.2 Notice the Wonder and Complexity of Life

What gives you a sense of wonder and awe? Are you amazed at the life of animals or perhaps how the earth rotates and circles around the sun? Do sunrises and sunsets impress you? Reflect on what you find to be remarkable about your observations of nature? Have you stopped to watch a rainbow or a storm passing through? What amazes you about life? Can you list several examples?

What gives you a sense of wonder and awe? List 10 things here.

1. _____

2. _____

3. _____

4. _____

5. _____

6. _____

7. _____

8. _____

9. _____

10. _____

What does this list say about you and what matters to you?

_____

_____

_____

_____

_____

_____

_____

3. Remind Yourself of the Briefness of Life

Life is short. We all know this is true, but we often do not quite believe it for ourselves or for those we care deeply about. For young and healthy people, in particular, they may feel that life will continue on forever and that they are immortal to some degree (Hazlitt, 1827). They may vaguely know that everyone will die sometime and someday. However, if they are generally young and healthy, they may not think they should pay much attention to this reality for many years or even for many decades to come. Older people often say that life goes by quickly as they age. They frequently try to warn younger people of this important realization, but it may not penetrate their awareness while they are still young with so much life expected ahead of them. However, sudden loss and trauma, such as losing a friend or younger family member to suicide, an accident, or a terminal illness, typically awakens their view that life can be short indeed.

If we find ways to remind ourselves that life is short, we may be better equipped to view life as sacred and to embrace the sacred in all things. We are better able to keep our priorities in mind, worry less about insignificant challenges or hassles, and not take some stressors as seriously as we often do. If life is short, we are more likely to seize every moment and follow paths that lead us to matters and people who are important to us. Recognizing that our time on earth is brief can help us to experience and find the divine and the sacred in all things. Every minute of life becomes more important and perhaps sacred when you know how short life really is.

Exercise 2.3 Reflection on the Shortness of Life

Do you have an older person in your life who has been a relative, loved one, mentor, or coworker? If so, could you talk with them about how life has gone for them and what their views might be on the shortness of life? Could you engage them in a conversation that asked them to reflect on their life path and the speed that it has accelerated as they aged? Once completed, what have you learned from your conversation? What insights can you gather from talking to these elders? Write it down here.

_____

_____

_____

_____

Exercise 2.4 Further Reflection on the Shortness of Life

Given that life expectancy is currently close to 80 years old in the developed world, with modest variations based on gender, geographic location, and other factors, can you calculate how much expected time you might have to your life? Is the majority of your life behind you rather than in front of you? How might you want to spend your remaining years knowing that you have a limited amount of life left and it is uncertain not only how long you will live but what your health and other life conditions might be for you in the future? What insights do you have after this reflection? How might you want to change, if at all, your approach to life as you realize that your time is limited?

Assuming you will live until 80 (a very general assumption for sure), how many more years would you have to live? _____

How would you ideally like to spend the rest of your life assuming practicalities (e.g., income) were not an important consideration?

_____

_____

How might you want to change, if at all, your approach to life as you realize that your time is limited?

_____

_____

_____

4. Put Yourself in Another's Shoes

It is easier to see the sacred in others if you can put yourself in the other person's shoes. This is helpful not only when considering other people but also when reflecting on the life of other nonhuman creatures too (e.g., animals). Putting yourself in the shoes or bodies of others, human or otherwise, is likely to give you pause and experience the sacredness and importance of all. The Golden Rule, popular among many religious and spiritual traditions, highlights this notion by stating that we should treat others as we wish to be treated (Gensler, 2013; Wattles, 1996).

Various and well-established cognitive behavioral techniques such as guided imagery (Utay & Miller, 2006) as well as gestalt techniques (Wollants, 2012) can help us better see ourselves within others. In doing so, it becomes easier to see the sacred and specialness of others, and it makes it harder to objectify or demonize others as well.

Exercise 2.5 Reflecting on Being in Another Person's Skin

Think about a person that you might have little in common with and may not like. Perhaps it is a coworker, relative, neighbor, or somebody that you interact with, even a stranger, customer, or someone you see periodically as you go about your daily life. Maybe it is a homeless person who asks for money at the entrance of a store. Select someone and then close your eyes and visualize them. Imagine that you are them and that you are living within them. How does it feel? How do you think others view them? How do you think they wish others would treat them? How do you understand how they became who they are?

Name someone who you do not like here _____

After visualizing living in their skin, how do you feel? _____

How might others treat you while living in their skin?

_____

How do you think they become the person that they are?

_____

_____

_____

What have you noticed about your reactions and reflection as you visualize being someone else, especially someone who you do not like at all?

_____

_____

_____

_____

5. Reflect on the Consequences of a Nonsacred Focused Life

Experiencing the world, and all creatures both human and nonhuman who inhabit it, with a sense of sacredness while finding the divine in all things offers a variety of healthy and productive consequences (Demerath, 2000; Grogan, 2021). The world becomes more special, important, valued, and accessible to one's love and respect. A nonsacred world makes it easier to objectify and even demonize others. A nonsacred world means that it might be okay to disrespect and neglect the needs and desires of others. Looking at the world through a sacred versus nonsacred lens might be like seeing the world in black and light versus Technicolor.

One common question we might ask ourselves when we reflect upon our challenges and conflicts in relationships is, "How did that work out for you?" When we do not see the sacred in others and perhaps behave in rude, disrespectful, and mean-spirited ways, things rarely turn out well for us. So often people will react and respond with anger and disrespect, which escalates into conflict, resulting in an undesirable outcome.

Exercise 2.6 Reflection on Everyone as Your Relative

Spend a day reflecting on every interaction that you have with someone who is your close relative, such as a sibling, child, parent, and so forth. As you observe or interact with others for a day, remind yourself that they are your close relative. How do you experience them with this mindset? Do you interact with them differently? Do you view them with a lens that is more positive? If you are a person of religious faith, can you try the same exercise but this time see the divine within everyone? Can you experience each person you interact with or observe as Jesus, Allah, God, the Great Spirit, or whatever your religious and spiritual perspective would suggest? How does that alter the way you view and interact with them? Write your reflections here.

_____

_____

_____

_____

What have you learned from this exercise? How does this perspective alter the way you view and interact with others? If you feel that it has helped you interact with others better, can you keep it going?

_____

_____

_____

_____

A Personal Example

When my son, Zach, was very young, I wanted him to develop the notion that the divine and sacred were in all things, including people, animals, and insects. I was attentive to the messages that he was learning as a young child and tried to highlight this notion in our daily activities. When we would find a spider in the house, for example, my son and I would try to capture the spider to put it outside rather than killing it. When we would find a snail in the garden chomping on our plants, we would move the snail to a different part of the garden rather than killing it. When doing so, I would remind my son that life is sacred. Now at age 27, Zach still takes spiders outside. The message stuck and he views creatures of all kinds with respect and the sense of sacredness, far surpassing his parents' own appreciation. As he moves the spider or snail, he always calls them "friends." This strategy has worked with his interaction with humans as well, and he tends to get along with and likes just about everyone.

Conclusion

Finding or seeing the divine or sacred in all things is an important and helpful way of viewing the world, including everyone and everything in it. This perspective is supported in many different religious and spiritual traditions and is highlighted in Jesuit spirituality and sensibilities (Carls, 2017; Hellwig, 1994; Taylor, 2017). Seeing the divine and sacred in all can be integrated into a wide range of situations when we experience problems and conflicts. It is a go-to tool for anyone (Pargament, 2011; Sandage & Strawn, 2022). It perhaps might be the most important of all the principles discussed in this book. If you truly see the sacred in all, then you cannot help but treat people with more compassion, respect, and attention. It becomes hard to demonize others. Certainly, there are many people who we do not like or want to be around. They are sacred too, even if their behavior, attitudes, or perspectives are problematic and even offensive. We do not have to like or agree with everyone, but perhaps we would do ourselves and others a favor if we could at least respect them as sacred beings.

Further Reading

Grogan, B. (2021). *Finding God in all things*. Messenger Publications.

Healey, C. J. (2014). *Praying with the Jesuits: Finding God in all things*. Paulist Press.

Howell, A. O. (1988). *The dove in the stone: Finding the sacred in the commonplace*. Quest Books.

Taylor, B. B. (2017). *An altar in the World: Finding the sacred beneath our feet*. Canterbury Press.

References

Carls, R. (2017). Finding God in all things: Panentheistic features in the Spiritual Exercises of St. Ignatius. *Gregorianum, 98*(4), 747–761.

Corbett, L. (2011). *The sacred cauldron: Psychotherapy as a spiritual practice*. Chiron Publications.

Demerath, III, N. J. (2000). The varieties of sacred experience: Finding the sacred in a secular grove. *Journal for the scientific study of religion, 39*(1), 1–11.

Emmons, R. A. (2005). Striving for the sacred: Personal goals, life meaning, and religion. *Journal of Social Issues, 61*(4), 731–745.

Engler, S., & Gardiner, M. Q. (2017). Semantics and the sacred. *Religion, 47*(4), 616–640.

Gensler, H. J. (2013). *Ethics and the golden rule*. Routledge.

Griffith, J. L., & Griffith, M. E. (Eds.). (2003). *Encountering the sacred in psychotherapy: How to talk with people about their spiritual lives.* Guilford Press.

Hazlitt, W. (1827). *On the feeling of immortality in youth.* Wm. Benton.

Healey, C. J. (2014). *Praying with the Jesuits: Finding God in all things.* Paulist Press.

Hellwig, M. K. (1994). Finding God in all things: A spirituality for today. *Sojourners,* 50–58.

Hölldobler, B., & Wilson, E. O. (1990). *The ants.* Belknap Press of Harvard University Press.

Jones, C. T., Collins, K., & Haley, T. L. (2021). "We lost to sushi": Why *My Octopus Teacher* is our win, too. *Journal of Literary & Cultural Disability Studies, 15*(4), 493–497.

Oxhandler, H. K. (2017). Namaste theory: A quantitative grounded theory on religion and spirituality in mental health treatment. *Religions, 8*(9), 168.

Pargament, K. I. (2011). *Spiritually integrated psychotherapy: Understanding and addressing the sacred.* Guilford Press.

Ross, N. (2021). *My Octopus Teacher,* posthumanism, and posthuman education: A pedagogical conceptualization. *Journal of Curriculum Theorizing, 36*(2), 1–15.

Sandage, S. J., & Strawn, B. D. (2022). *Spiritual diversity in psychotherapy: Engaging the sacred in clinical practice.* American Psychological Association.

Sharma, R., Kumar, A., & Koushal, V. (2021). Namaste—"I bow to the divine in you." *International Journal of Medicine and Public Health, 11*(1), 63–64.

Simard, J., & Volicer, L. (2010). Effects of Namaste Care on residents who do not benefit from usual activities. *American Journal of Alzheimer's Disease & Other Dementias®, 25*(1), 46–50.

Taylor, B. B. (2017). *An altar in the World: Finding the sacred beneath our feet.* Canterbury Press.

Thys, T. M. (2020). Exploring eight-armed intelligence through film. *Animal Sentience, 4*(26), 27.

Utay, J., & Miller, M. (2006). Guided imagery as an effective therapeutic technique: A brief review of its history and efficacy research. *Journal of Instructional Psychology, 33*(1), 40–43.

Wattles, J. (1996). *The golden rule.* Oxford University Press.

Wilson, E. O. (1963). The social biology of ants. *Annual Review of Entomology, 8*(1), 345–368.

Wilson, E. O. (1988). Ants (Hymenoptera: Formicidae). In J. K. Liebherr, *Zoogeography of Caribbean insects* (p. 214). Comstock.

Wollants, G. (2012). *Gestalt therapy: Therapy of the situation.* Sage.

CHAPTER 3

Cura Personalis

Care for the Whole Person

An important and popular element of Jesuit spirituality, also frequently found in various ways within other religious and spiritual traditions, is the notion of *cura personalis*, a Latin phrase meaning "care of the whole person" (DePergola, 2019; Kolvenbach, 2007; McGinn, 2015). In today's increasingly specialized world, the notion of caring for the *whole* person often gets lost. So often, we have become specialists and subspecialists conducting our interactions with others via a narrow lens and framework (Haber, 1995). For example, over the years there are many fewer general practitioners in such professional fields as psychology, medicine, and law. As these fields mature and develop, specialization becomes the norm. In doing so, an unintended consequence is that we may miss the whole person or the big picture.

You may be familiar with the popular Buddhist parable about several blind men touching different parts of an elephant in such a way that they draw very different conclusions about the creature that vary dramatically based on their limited experience of the animal (Saxe, 2016). Specialization can result in a similarly narrow focus of attention and understanding that fail to appreciate the whole (Arthur, 2004). *Cura personalis* highlights the need to see the whole person.

The Unintended Consequences of Specialization

It is certainly understandable that in many fields people feel compelled to specialize. Since there is so much information to absorb in so many professions, it has become a necessity to stay within one's area of limited expertise and training and thus limit one's professional activities in general to increasingly narrow areas of focus (Arthur, 2004). Mental health professionals, for example, might attempt to specialize in somewhat general ways, such as working with children, teens, or adults or focusing their professional efforts on particular types of psychotherapy such as psychoanalysis, family systems approaches, cognitive behavioral therapy, or marital or group therapy. However, these professionals are increasingly sub-specializing even further, such as using dialectical behavior therapy for borderline personality, neuropsychological assessment for attention-deficit/hyperactivity disorder, or applied behavioral analysis for autism spectrum disorder. They may also focus their clinical work on highly specialized treatments regimens (e.g., mindfulness-based stress reduction, eye movement desensitization reprocessing) as well. While specialization is a reasonable and expected pathway for mature and advanced fields with a great deal of evidence-based guidelines, we all must be vigilant to keep the whole person in mind and not lose track that we are treating a complicated and real person.

Additionally, our litigious society also suggests that professionals should be careful not to dabble in areas outside of their expertise for fear of malpractice claims or other litigation against them (Barnett, 2008). However, perhaps an unintended consequence and potential disadvantage of this level of increasing specialization is the problem that occurs when a blind man touches the elephant and comes up with erroneous conclusions about the animal since they are unable to focus on the big picture or on the whole creature. This is where the notion and wisdom of *cura personalis* becomes especially relevant and important.

The Problem with Dualism

An additional problem in trying to embrace *cura personalis* is the long-standing tradition and error of separating our physical bodies from our psychosocial ones. For centuries, a mind-body dualism existed in that physical and psychological problems were typically considered separate and dichotomized as issues of either the body or concerns of the mind (Burgmer & Forstmann, 2018; Forstmann & Burgmer, 2015; Forstmann et al., 2012). The popular and centuries-old biomedical approach to disease, health, and wellness often meant that symptoms were categorized into oversimplified distinct and separate biological or psychological categories (Deacon, 2013). This still occurs today even though research provides clear documentation and evidence that the biomedical model has numerous problems and is not supported by current quality research and best professional practice (Sheridan & Radmacher, 1992).

The Biopsychosocial Model

This frequent challenge of missing the big and holistic picture was addressed in a landmark article published in *Science* by University of Rochester psychiatrist George Engel, who introduced the *biopsychosocial* model (Engel, 1977). It argued that medical and psychiatric problems could be better considered and treated if a biopsychosocial rather than biomedical model was used to diagnose and treat them. This important and groundbreaking paper led to greater efforts in health care for treating the whole person by considering the complex interplay of biological, psychological, and social factors in contributing to the development and treatment of a wide variety of health-related problems (Adler, 2009; Suls & Rothman, 2004). However, the biopsychosocial model is not *cura personalis* or whole person enough since it does not necessarily consider spiritual matters. If we add spirituality to the biopsychosocial model, we get the *biopsychosocialspiritual* model that better reflects the wisdom and spirit of *cura personalis* (Hefti, 2013; Katerndahl & Oyiriaru, 2007). Biopsychosocialspiritual is a mouthful, but maintaining this point of view and perspective likely is a more accurate way of thinking about health, illness, and wellness (Klawonn et al., 2019).

An important and additional concept that should be introduced that fits well with the biopsychosocial or biopsycosocialspiritual model is systems theory (Brown, 2010; Gray et al., 1976). Systems theory suggests that when there is change in one important area of a person's life then we can likely expect a ripple effect that can cause change in other areas of a person's life. This theory is consistent with the "butterfly effect" suggestion that an apparently small and insignificant change in one part of the world can have a ripple effect that affects changes in other parts of the world (Lorenz, 2000; Palmer et al., 2014; Vernon, 2017). A good example of the butterfly effect is a wildfire, an earthquake, or a volcanic eruption in one part of the globe having an enormous impact thousands of miles away. A wildfire or volcanic eruption can create poor air quality and darkened skies thousands of miles away while an underwater earthquake can cause a massive tsunami across the globe. The butterfly effect can also be applied to people. Someone might be depressed and then find excuses not to go to work, ultimately losing their job, their income, and important relationships. Someone might develop a significant mental illness such as schizophrenia, bipolar, or a substance abuse problem and then their life spirals down in various ways ultimately leading to homelessness. On the more positive side, someone might lose weight through diet and exercise that leads to enthusiastic compliments from friends, family, and coworkers that ultimately increases self-confidence leading to improved mood, relationship satisfaction, and job performance. Systems theory should thus be considered with the biopsychosocialspiritual model to effectively care for the whole person in a *cura personalis* manner.

Let us examine how *cura personalis* and related concepts such as the biopsychosocialspiritual model and systems theory can be helpful in developing and nurturing this important life principle.

Case Example 3.1 Fatima

Fatima was referred for emergency weight loss by her internal medicine physician. She desperately needed to lose weight to survive. She had significant sleep apnea and, in combination with her obesity, was at high risk for immediate death. Her doctor admitted her to a behavioral medicine psychiatric unit at a university medical center since her risk of death was so significant and immediate in his view. Her doctor wanted to put her on a closely medically supervised restrictive diet as soon as possible and have her sleep carefully monitored in a hospital setting as well.

Fatima was uncooperative with the psychologist on the unit. She did not want to talk with "a shrink" and was resistant to all efforts for any mental health diagnostic or treatment services. She was originally from another country and culture that frowned upon receiving any type of psychiatric care. She wanted to be treated as a medical patient only and did not want to acknowledge any psychological or behavioral influence associated with her health problems or hospitalization. Over several weeks, Fatima warmed up to the psychologist on the unit who would check in with her daily and try to develop a friendly relationship. Finally, she agreed to talk with the psychologist and after several conversations admitted that she was hoping to die from her sleep apnea. She was depressed and experienced some challenging family difficulties and stressors that made living painful for her. Since she was a religious woman, she vowed not to actively kill herself but thought that dying in her sleep would be an ideal way to go. Since she was already in her 60s, she felt that she had lived a long enough life anyway.

Over several weeks of daily and sometimes several-times-a-day conversations, Fatima agreed to discuss her life and troubles in more detail and came to enjoy her conversations with the psychologist. They worked through many of the issues that deeply distressed her, and they integrated family members into some of these conversations as well. She ultimately lost weight and returned to the hospital unit eight months after discharge sporting a new outfit that highlighted her weight loss and her new lease on life. She was grateful for the services she received and hugged the psychologist when she saw him on the unit.

While Fatima was initially treated as a medical patient who needed to lose weight to avoid death from sleep apnea, when her whole person was fully considered, including taking her depression, religious identity and beliefs, and family troubles into consideration, her prognosis improved, and she cooperated with the treatment plan. Using the biopsychosocialspiritual and *cura personalis* approach rather than a narrow biomedical approach likely saved her life.

Case Example 3.2 Maria

Maria is anxious and has frequent panic attacks. Her fears have resulted in her never working outside of the home or traveling beyond a few hours away from her hometown. Her husband, whom she met and dated in high school, has always accepted her fears and has graciously accommodated them. Her internal medicine physician prescribed Xanax and over time she became dependent on the medication for her day-to-day functioning. Her physician referred her to a psychiatrist for further care. He hoped that a psychiatrist would be better able to get her to manage her medication more appropriately. Maria did not feel very comfortable with the psychiatrist stating that he was a "cold fish" and not very friendly. She said that he made her nervous and that she took Xanax to calm herself down before her appointments with him. In frustration, the psychiatrist referred her to a psychologist stating that she was a "difficult patient" and not adequately complying with his treatment plan.

Maria was nervous when meeting the psychologist and admitted that she took Xanax before their initial meeting. During several sessions, Maria admitted that she had a difficult childhood with an abusive mother and an absent father and experienced a very guilt-ridden and highly conservative religious upbringing. She reported that many people in her family had anxiety and panic problems and that most of them abused alcohol to deal with their distress. She admitted that she drank heavily as well. Her anxiety prevented her from doing many activities and she would only leave the home when she was with her husband, who was also her driver, as she never learned to drive.

Over time, Maria agreed to try a variety of cognitive behavioral strategies for better coping, and her husband was included in some of the sessions to discuss how he could support her efforts to become more functional and independent. She was also referred to a kindly cleric within her faith tradition to help her manage and cope better with the religious guilt that further fueled her anxieties. She gradually decreased her Xanax consumption with medical supervision and relied more heavily on cognitive behavioral strategies as well as spiritual direction from the cleric.

Treating Maria's Xanax addiction and anxiety was better served with a *cura personalis* perspective. Her physicians with a biomedical model of treatment initially sought to help her only by prescribing medication for her anxiety and panic. The medication became part of the problem as she increasingly relied on the drug to help her get through her days. A *cura personalis* approach gave her many more tools to better deal with anxiety and panic so that her need for medication was eventually eliminated.

Fatima and Maria were initially treated by their health care providers with a singular biomedical model in mind. Behavioral and psychological difficulties were thought by both professionals and referral sources alike to be best treated with a medical approach only. The reverse is also a common problem in that mental health professionals may often overlook biological, medical, or spiritual factors focusing on psychosocial causes only. This unidimensional approach was clearly inadequate to address the complexities of their troubles, and a more biopsychosocialspiritual and *cura personalis* approach proved transformative and even lifesaving in these cases. Fatima and Maria are not unusual examples at all. They represent many cases frequently presented to both medical and mental health professionals. Too often, a simple approach is selected to deal with a complex problem and being always mindful of a biopsychosocialspiritual and *cura personalis* perspective usually will provide intervention that is more helpful.

In the next section, we will consider several important strategies to better provide *cura personalis* approaches to our lives.

Four Strategies to Better Nurture *Cura Personalis* into Our Lives

To best nurture and highlight a *cura personalis* approach to life, several strategies and techniques can be helpful to keep in mind.

1. Filter All That We Do through a Biopsychosocialspiritual Lens

It is easy for us all to fall back on our narrow range of focus, interests, and expertise when living our lives. We tend to see the world through the lens of what we know or what makes us feel most comfortable and confident. You are likely familiar with the phrase "when someone has a hammer, they tend to see nails everywhere" (e.g., Adalı et al., 2018). We all may do this depending upon our interests and expertise. Thus, our experience and worldviews about human nature and behavior will likely provide the framework for how we view our lives and those of others.

While it is certainly important to stay within our lane of competence and expertise, we need to be mindful of the biopsychosocialspiritual model. As we have illustrated with several case examples, caring for the whole person means being aware of the interplay of biological, psychological, social, and spiritual factors that interact in various and often complex ways to create the situation and environment in which we live. We can acknowledge these multiple influences on human behavior and challenges.

Exercise 3.1 Wearing Biopsychosocialspiritual Lens

Now that you have been introduced to the biopsycosocialspiritual model, let's see if you can use it with yourself and people that you know. Reflect on a challenge or difficulty you are currently experiencing in life. Perhaps you are dealing with relationship or work stress, or maybe you are caring for a family member who is ill or either very young or old. Maybe you are struggling with a medical or psychological problem. Write down in four separate categories (i.e., biological, psychological, social, and spiritual) the influences that these elements have on your current problem. For example, a biological influence might include lack of sleep or time for exercise or perhaps dealing with medication side effects. Psychological influences might include anxiety, depression, low self-confidence, and stress. Social influences might include conflict with coworkers or family members or perhaps not meeting the expectations of others including society's. Spiritual influences might include feeling distant from God or the divine, lack of meaning and purpose in life, or confusion about what path, traditions, or rituals to follow. Look over your list of influences for the four categories.

Biopsychosocialspiritual Influences on a Current Problems or Issue in Your Life

Biological _____

Psychological _____

Social _____

Spiritual _____

Now how can you address them in a way that offers balance and attention to all four elements of your life? What elements are being ignored or not attended to? Can you come up with a plan to address those elements that are being neglected? For example, getting more exercise, talking through a conflict with a coworker or family member, decreeing your social media use so that you minimize comparing yourself with others, starting a prayer routine?

Biopsychosocialspiritual Strategies for Better Coping in Your Life

Biological   _____

Psychological   _____

Social   _____

Spiritual   _____

What have you learned about caring for your whole self through this exercise?

_____

Can you implement your insights to care for the whole you?

_____

What might get in the way of doing so?

_____

2. Consult with Others with Perspectives and Expertise Different Than Our Own

Given the limitations of our perspectives and expertise, it is important to speak to others who offer perspectives and competencies different from our own. Care of the whole person or *cura personalis* can work better if we bring multiple strategies, expertise, and perspectives to the table considering various ways we can fully care for our whole selves.

Exercise 3.2 Consultation with Others

What expertise do you lack in caring for your whole self or perhaps the whole self of others? As you consider the biological, psychological, social, and spiritual aspects of yourself and perhaps those others who are important to you, what elements or categories do you tend to lack expertise in? For example, you may feel that you lack much needed knowledge and perspective in any one of these elements such as biological/medical or spiritual/religious areas?

What needed expertise or skills do you lack? Write them down here.

Biopsychosocialspiritual Expertise or Skills That You Nneed but Lack in Your Life

Biological   _____

Psychological   _____

Social   _____

Spiritual   _____

Once you have identified an area that you know little about given your skill sets and needs, can you find someone to consult with to help you fill in the gaps? Maybe you want to consult with a physician or nurse about a biological concern or maybe you want to talk with a cleric about a religious or spiritual issue. Identify someone who can help you better understand and act on a need in one of the four categories from our biopsychosocialspiritual model. Who would you consult with under each category?

Biopsychosocialspiritual Expertise or Skills That You Need but Lack in Your Life

Biological   _____

Psychological   _____

Social   _____

Spiritual   _____

Once you talk with the identified person, write down what you learned and how you might apply it to your life or those around you.

_____

_____

_____

_____

3. Maintain Humility with Our Biopsychosocialspiritual Whole Person Tools

Humility is not a characteristic that is often valued in contemporary society but is needed perhaps more than ever to embrace *cura personalis* and a biopsychosocialspiritual perspective. Admitting that we have many limitations and are not able to fully understand and appreciate all aspects of our lives and those who we are closest to can be a hard pill to swallow for many of us. Yet, humility keeps us from overreaching and allows us to better care for ourselves and others too (Davis et al., 2021; Gordon, 2018). These tools and perspectives have their limitations. These tools may not alter the problems of racism and discrimination or provide adequate housing or financial stability, for example.

Exercise 3.3 Getting in Touch with Humility

What qualities that you value do you lack? Do you lack expertise that you wished you had? Do you have elements of your personality that you, or others around you, are not satisfied with? Are you quick tempered? Do you tend to feel slighted easily? Do you tend to get depressed often? Do you place too high demands or expectations on others? What would your critics say about you? Are there people in your life who do not like you? Can you ask someone who knows you very well what your faults might be?

While this exercise is not meant to depress you or make you feel guilty, it is helpful to have a more realistic view of ourselves including our faults. Once you engage in this exercise, write down these faults and parts of you that are not so good. Perhaps rate them in order of significance. Can you highlight those items that you feel you are willing to work on later?

List at least five qualities that you lack that you wished you had or were better at

1. _____

2. _____

3. _____

4. _____

5. _____

Now circle the items that you feel you would like to work on? Do you think you can make progress on the circled items? Why or why not?

_____

_____

4. Treat Others as We Wish to Be Treated Ourselves

You are likely familiar with the Golden Rule. It states that we should treat others as we wish to be treated ourselves (Gensler, 2013; Wattles, 1996). Another strategy to support a *cura personalis* perspective is to remind ourselves of the Golden Rule and thus to treat others as we wish to be treated. When we reflect on our own issues, troubles, relationships, and so forth, we can more easily see the complexity and the multiple factors that contribute to who we are and what challenges we face ourselves. We know that we are not unidimensional and need multiple approaches to manage our lives and troubles. Constantly reminding ourselves of the Golden Rule and committing ourselves to it can help us to carry out *cura personalis* work with all our clients and better appreciate the complexities in their lives and treatment needs.

Exercise 3.4 Practicing the Golden Rule

List the five people in your life that you dislike the most. Perhaps there is a coworker, family member, colleague, neighbor, or others who you interact with that you really do not like or want to be around. Maybe there are some people in your life that you have been rude to or have ignored. Perhaps there are some who you refuse to talk to, you have ghosted, or you have exchanged angry words with.

List five people who you dislike the most

1. _____

2. _____

3. _____

4. _____

5. _____

Review your list and ask yourself how you might treat them if you were them. If you could live in their shoes, how would you wish to be treated by you? Write your response here.

_____

_____

_____

_____

_____

What insights have you found from this exercise? Does it offer you an opportunity to alter the way you interact with these individuals? Why or why not?

_____

_____

_____

_____

Conclusion

Our increasingly specialized world may lend itself to avoid interacting with others using a whole person biopsychosocialspiritual or *cura personalis* perspective. Jesuit spirituality, as well as spirituality among other traditions, warns us to avoid this problem and potential trap of seeing and treating others in a narrowly focused, unidimensional, and restricted manner. While most of us have limited tools to use in our life given our experience and areas of specialization, if we are aware of whole-person approaches, we can at least recognize where they might be needed and refer to appropriate resources to manage various aspects of our lives and those of others.

Combining the materials presented in Chapters 2 and 3, it is easier to engage in and highlight *cura personalis* work when we also view ourselves and others as sacred, seeing the divine or sacred in all. Therefore, as we go through the various elements of spiritually based life principles introduced and articulated in each subsequent chapter, we want to add and integrate these themes and tools into a consistent whole. Combining a sacred view of others (Chapter 2 material) along with a *cura personalis* perspective (Chapter 3 material) can work synergistically, offering a more thoughtful and spiritually based approach to our lives. In subsequent chapters, we will add more elements to our spiritually based principles approach adding additional tools and richness to the process.

Further Reading

Engel, G. L. (1977). The need for a new medical model: A challenge for biomedicine. *Science, 196*(4286), 129–136.

Klawonn, A., Kernan, D., & Lynskey, J. (2019). A 5-week seminar on the biopsychosocial-spiritual model of self-care improves anxiety, self-compassion, mindfulness, depression, and stress in graduate healthcare students. *International Journal of Yoga Therapy, 29*(1), 81–89.

Kolvenbach, P.-H. (2007). "Cura personalis." *Review of Ignatian Spirituality, 38*(1), 9–17.

McGinn, A., S.J. (2015). Mission matters: What do Jesuits mean by *cura personalis*? *Conversations on Jesuit Higher Education, 47*(1), 10.

Plante, T. G. (2016). Principles of incorporating spirituality into professional clinical practice. *Practice Innovations, 1*(4), 276–281.

References

Adalı, T., Trussell, H. J., Hansen, L. K., & Calhoun, V. D. (2018). The dangers of following trends in research: Sparsity and other examples of hammers in search of nails. *Proceedings of the IEEE, 106*(6), 1014–1018.

Adler, R. H. (2009). Engel's biopsychosocial model is still relevant today. *Journal of psychosomatic research, 67*(6), 607–611.

Arthur, A. R. (2004). Work-related stress, the blind men and the elephant. *British Journal of Guidance & Counselling, 32*(2), 157–169.

Barnett, J. E. (2008). The ethical practice of psychotherapy: Easily within our reach. *Journal of Clinical Psychology, 64*(5), 569–575.

Brown, J. (2010). Psychotherapy integration: Systems theory and self-psychology. *Journal of Marital and Family Therapy, 36*(4), 472–485.

Burgmer, P., & Forstmann, M. (2018). Mind-body dualism and health revisited: How belief in dualism shapes health behavior. *Social Psychology, 49*(4), 219–230.

Davis, E. B., Plante, T. G., Grey, M. J., Kim, C. L., Freeman-Coppadge, D., Lefevor, G. T., Paulez, J. A., Giwa, S., Lasser, J., Stratton, S. P., Deneke, E., & Glowiak, K. (2021). The role of civility and cultural humility in navigating controversial areas in psychology. *Spirituality in Clinical Practice, 8*(2), 79–87.

Deacon, B. J. (2013). The biomedical model of mental disorder: A critical analysis of its validity, utility, and effects on psychotherapy research. *Clinical psychology review, 33*(7), 846–861.

DePergola, P. A., II. (2019). The *cura personalis* of healthcare delivery: Ethical reflections on internal medicine. *Online Journal of Health Ethics*, *15*(1), 2.

Engel, G. L. (1977). The need for a new medical model: A challenge for biomedicine. *Science*, *196*(4286), 129–136.

Forstmann, M., & Burgmer, P. (2015). Adults are intuitive mind-body dualists. *Journal of Experimental Psychology: General*, *144*(1), 222–235.

Forstmann, M., Burgmer, P., & Mussweiler, T. (2012). "The mind is willing, but the flesh is weak": The effects of mind-body dualism on health behavior. *Psychological Science*, *23*(10), 1239–1245.

Gensler, H. J. (2013). *Ethics and the golden rule*. Routledge.

Gordon, E. C. (2018). Intellectual humility, spirituality, and counselling. *Journal of psychology and theology*, *46*(4), 279–291.

Gray, W., Cochran, D., & Gray, L. R. (1976). General systems theory in psychotherapy. *International Journal of Offender Therapy and Comparative Criminology*, *20*(2), 107–116.

Haber, S. (1995). Specialization in psychotherapy: From psychotherapist to psychooncologist. *Professional Psychology: Research and Practice*, *26*(4), 427–432.

Hefti, R. (2013). The Extended Biopsychosocial Model: A whole-person-approach to psychosomatic medicine and psychiatry. *Psyche & Geloof*, *24*(2), 119–129.

Katerndahl, D., & Oyiriaru, D. (2007). Assessing the biopsychosociospiritual model in primary care: Development of the biopsychosociospiritual inventory (BioPSSI). *The International Journal of Psychiatry in Medicine*, *37*(4), 393–414.

Klawonn, A., Kernan, D., & Lynskey, J. (2019). A 5-week seminar on the biopsychosocial-spiritual model of self-care improves anxiety, self-compassion, mindfulness, depression, and stress in graduate healthcare students. *International Journal of Yoga Therapy*, *29*(1), 81–89.

Kolvenbach, P.-H. (2007). "Cura personalis." *Review of Ignatian Spirituality*, *38*(1), 9–17.

Lorenz, E. (2000). The butterfly effect. *World Scientific Series on Nonlinear Science Series A*, *39*, 91–94.

McGinn, A., S.J. (2015). Mission matters: What do Jesuits mean by *cura personalis*? *Conversations on Jesuit Higher Education*, *47*(1), 10.

Palmer, T. N., Döring, A., & Seregin, G. (2014). The real butterfly effect. *Nonlinearity*, *27*(9), R123.

Saxe, J. G. (2016). *The blind men and the elephant*. Enrich Spot Limited.

Sheridan, C. L., & Radmacher, S. A. (1992). *Health psychology: Challenging the biomedical model*. John Wiley & Sons.

Suls, J., & Rothman, A. (2004). Evolution of the biopsychosocial model: Prospects and challenges for health psychology. *Health Psychology*, *23*(2), 119–125.

Vernon, J. L. (2017). Understanding the butterfly effect. *American Scientist*, *105*(3), 130.

Wattles, J. (1996). *The golden rule*. Oxford University Press.

CHAPTER 4

Discernment

Embracing the Four *D*s

Life is often ultimately about decision making. We may wonder if we should leave our job or marriage or how to better manage relationships with family, friends, neighbors, and coworkers. We might be struggling with gripping depression, anxiety, or addictions and seek better ways to work through these difficulties. We may wonder how to find more satisfaction in life or potentially risk certain securities and comforts to follow our dreams and aspirations. We may wonder if our life is still worth living at all. We also might be trying to assist others in talking through and processing difficult and often conflicting feelings, thoughts, and behaviors to make choices in life that will be healthier, more productive, and more satisfying.

Jesuit spirituality offers a great deal when it comes to thoughtful decision making. The 500-year-old process of discernment through *The Spiritual Exercises of St. Ignatius* is well known and has been adopted by many people and groups regardless of their spiritual or religious affiliations or interests (Buckley, 1973; Futrell, 1970; Lienhard, 1980). Discernment is defined as a process of making sound, wise, and thoughtful judgements (Gula, 1997; Liebert, 2008). In Jesuit and other religious contexts, it highlights the strategies used to determine and follow God's (or the divine's) will for one's life. It involves a "discernment of spirits" in seeking to find a calling or direction inspired by and being in touch with spiritual, religious, and other sources (Buckley, 1973; Futrell, 1970). Used either in a spiritual or in a secular manner, discernment is an organized and stepwise structured process for making important and hopefully positive decisions.

A "discernment of spirits" speaks to the notion that the divine, as understood by each person, has a plan for each one of us. It suggests that there is a path forward in our decision making that is consistent with God's will for us following religious, spiritual, and moral guidelines (Buckley, 1973; Futrell, 1970). Many people report feeling called to certain actions or life paths. They feel that by being better in tune with a divine or sacred plan their resulting steps forward will feel right, appropriate, consoling, and even blessed. Attending to the discernment of spirits also suggests that consulting with thoughtful and knowledgeable others is critical in order to decide if the discernment process and resulting decisions are indeed following the right path (Plante, 2017, 2020).

In this chapter, I will focus on the four-step process of discernment that can be utilized by anyone and that offers a structured step-by-step process for decision making. Several examples and exercises will be provided as well.

The Four *D*s: Discovery, Detachment, Discernment, and Direction

The four *D*s refers to the discernment process that can be used in any environment or forum where thoughtful decision making and judgments are needed (Plante, 2017). The four *D*s refer to *discovery, detachment, discernment*, and *direction*. They are easy to use and remember and can be embraced by people of all ages and stages in life.

Discovery

The first step in the discernment process is to discover, articulate, and list one's gifts, talents, desires, and interests. While this might seem to be an easy and obvious task to complete, many people find it difficult to list these qualities for themselves. In fact, often it can be helpful to ask someone to consult with family, friends, coworkers, and others who know them well to assist them in listing their gifts and talents. Additionally, many people get so preoccupied and focused with the daily distractions and chores of life that they lose sight of their desires, dreams, and true talents.

We all can try to reflect on our gifts, talents, desires, and interests and to write them down and carefully review them. We might be surprised by what we can learn about ourselves as we go through this discovery process. Typically, we get in touch with parts of ourselves that have been put aside by the practicalities of life. Various distractions and other priorities get in the way, and old dreams, desires, and interests are too often forgotten or even repressed.

Case Example 4.1 Jen

Jen is a college senior who is majoring in business and minoring in art. She is a second-generation Vietnamese American as her parents fled Vietnam in the 1970s following the war there and found their way to the United States. Jen's parents, along with an older brother, operate a successful business, and the expectation of her family is that once Jen graduates from college, she will join the family business as her brother did several years ago after he completed his college degree in accounting.

Jen has always had a compelling artistic side to her but never really questioned her plans to join the family business after she graduates from college. As she sees her college years coming to an end and graduation right around the corner, she finds herself more and more depressed and anxious. She has trouble sleeping and did poorly on a recent examination, which was an unusual occurrence for her. After prompting from her roommate and from her boyfriend, she went to see her academic advisor on campus for advice.

Jen's advisor asked her to consider going through the discernment process and began with a discussion focused on the discovery of her gifts, talents, desires, and interests. Jen explained that she planned on working in the family business after graduation, but her advisor could detect that her heart was not really into this career plan and that she became more alive and activated when she talked about some of her art projects. When this observation was brought to Jen's attention, she said that her family discouraged her art interests as being frivolous and not practical enough to make a good living. Additionally, they believed that a business degree was worth the high cost of college tuition as well as the time investment to obtain a degree but that subjects such as art, music, and the humanities were not. Jen continued with the discovery process, listing her gifts and interests, and talking with several friends and a few professors she admired. In addition to her art interests, Jen discovered other gifts and talents that she was reintroduced to though the discovery process as well, such as music, dance, and fashion.

Case Example 4.2 Rod

Rod is an executive in his late 40s, has three teenage children, and has been married for 25 years. Rod considers himself a "solid citizen"—a churchgoing, moral person who proudly served in the military and is an Eagle Scout as well. Rod claims that he has been paid very well at his company but that his boss, many coworkers, and the culture of the company are all "a bit sleazy." He reports that they find ways to get around rules and regulations, never breaking the law but coming close to doing so. They also have a habit of not being truthful and fully transparent with their customers and with each other as well.

Rod got into a marital crisis when he went to a strip club with his boss and several coworkers that led to a sexual encounter with one of the workers at the club. Rod admits that he and his fellow coworkers had been drinking rather heavily and that "things just got out of hand." He was not going to mention this incident to his wife, but he felt compelled to do so when his wife returned from a routine doctor's appointment where medical testing revealed that she tested positive for the HPV virus. Rod figured that he must have passed the virus along to her after his sexual encounter at the strip club.

Rod acknowledged that he did not fit in at the company that he worked for but that his salary, benefits, work hours, and company location were all seductive, helping him to better afford his home, family needs, and lifestyle. Rod participated in the discernment process to help him decide what his next steps should be in terms of his career and life.

During the discovery portion of the discernment process, Rod got in touch with his conservation interests that were ignited and nurtured during his Boy Scout days in his youth. He loved scouting and found that the hiking and backpacking trips were transformative for him as he grew up in a city environment and in a family who had little interest in camping and backpacking. His Eagle Scout project was a conservation project that he was always proud of and would eagerly discuss when prompted to do so. Once Rod got married, started a family, and started working, he drifted away from these nature and conservation interests as demands of work and family life took all his time, attention, and energy. The discovery phase of discernment resulted in getting Rod interested once again in this important and core part of his life and the conservation interests they ignited.

The discovery process helped both Jen and Rod get more in touch with their truer interests, desires, and gifts that had been neglected or pushed aside by external factors such as expectations of others and the practicalities of life. Once they reignited these interests and desires, they were ready for the next stage in the discernment process, detachment.

Exercise 4.1 Discovering Your Gifts

What are your gifts? What do people say you are especially good at? Write them down. Make it as exhaustive as you can. What talents, skills, and interests do you have in all sorts of areas?

What Are Your Gifts, Talents, and Special Interests?

1. _____

2. _____

3. _____

4. _____

5. _____

6. _____

7. _____

8. _____

9. _____

10. _____

Any more to list?

_____

_____

Once you have completed your list, circle the items that you are especially proud of and perhaps underscore the ones that you would like to nurture and develop further. What has this exercise taught you about yourself? Write your reflections here:

_____

_____

_____

_____

Detachment

The second step in the discernment process is detachment. Detachment refers to finding ways to detach from all the influencing voices that encourage us to do, or not to do, certain things and sideline our true desires and interests. Family members, friends, or even expectations and messages from society at large all offer both subtle and not-so-subtle ideas and instructions about how we should live our lives and what we should do with our time and talents.

It is difficult to detach from the cacophony of voices all around us that pressure us to follow particular life paths or seek certain life goals. We all are vulnerable to both upward and downward social comparisons in that we evaluate our lives, activities, desires, resources, and so forth through the lens of observing others who we either envy or wish to avoid (Crusius et al., 2022; Suls & Wheeler, 2013; Suls & Wills, 1991). For example, if those around you are much wealthier than you, you will likely feel poor, while if you are surrounded by people much poorer than you are, you will likely feel rich. If those around you are highly educated, you will feel ignorant in comparison, and yet if you are surrounded by uneducated people, you will likely feel quite intelligent. As we compare ourselves to others in various ways, we will likely make decisions about pathways in our lives that may fit the expectations or values of others but not necessarily ourselves.

Jen, in the case presented above, is clearly influenced by the expectations of her family to pursue a practical business degree and then to join the family business after she graduates from college. Additionally, she is also influenced by her fellow business students and by society at-large to make a good living with a high salary after the significant financial and time investment of a college education. Rod, in the other case introduced above, also was following the expectations of his family, friends, and society to make a good living to support his family and their lifestyle even if he was working at a company and with people there that he felt were rather "sleazy."

Both Jen and Rod could benefit from spending some time detaching from these voices and influences to reflect further on how they might alter their life paths in a way that is more consistent with their perceived gifts, talents, desires, and interests rather than the influence and expectations of others. This process of detachment takes some time and effort since these outside voices and influences are so strong and constant. They can even be so subtle that we do not consciously recognize them. Jen and Rod should attempt to deflect all outside influences in their reflections on the next steps in their lives. Additionally, they could benefit from writing down what messages and expectations they hear from others versus what they hear from their own inner voice. This process helps to compartmentalize and privilege their own desires separated from those of others. With adequate detachment, they can attempt the next and most important stage, which highlights the difference between consolation and desolation in the discernment process.

Exercise 4.2 Detaching from the Influence of Others

Reflect on all the influencing voices in your life. They might include parents, coworkers, friends, neighbors, and society-at-large. What are these voices telling you to do with your life? Make a list of the most influential voices in your life. List these voices down. Next to each one, list what they want you to do with your life.

Influential Voices in Your Life　　　　　　　　　**What Are They Saying to You?**

1. _____

2. _____

3. _____

4. _____

5. _____

6. _____

7. _____

8. _____

9. _____

10. _____

Are there themes that emerge with these influential voices? Do they involve living and working in a certain way? Do issues of status, money, prestige, and fitting in with family, neighborhood, or society's expectations come up? Now, try to detach from these voices and messages. Take a moment and a deep breath to allow all those voices to go mute. What has this exercise taught you? What reflections do you have on your life when you mute the various voices telling you what to do and how to do it? Write them here.

_____

_____

_____

_____

_____

Exercise 4.3   Accepting Rejection and Disproval from Others

Think about doing whatever you wish without following the expectations of the important people and groups in your life that you listed in Exercise 4.2. Imagine that you rejected their advice and expectations to do what you felt you wanted to do. How would they react? Would they reject or abandon you? Imagine a conversation with these important others (e.g., parents, spouse, coworkers, neighbors, social media) as you describe your plans. Imagine their reactions. Write them down for each person here.

Influential Voices in Your Life	Their Reaction to Your Decisions
1. _____	
2. _____	

3. _____

4. _____

5. _____

6. _____

7. _____

8. _____

9. _____

10. _____

How do you feel as you imagine these interactions and scenarios? What would you say or do in response? Could you do this in real life? Why or why not?

_____

_____

_____

_____

_____

Discernment

The third step in the discernment process involves paying attention to what gives you consolation versus desolation (Bishop & Carlton, 2016; Dougherty, 2009; Liebert, 2008; Nancy, 2006). *Consolation* refers to reflecting on activities or paths that give you peace, solace, and comfort. *Desolation* refers to reflecting on the various activities or paths that make you feel uncomfortable, stressed, irritated, and uninspired. This ongoing reflection and discernment help to find a path that will ultimately lead more towards consolation rather than desolation. This process can be an ongoing one and is often enhanced by talking with supportive others who have your best interest in mind with no agenda for any particular outcome (Gula, 1997).

When Jen, in the example above, was encouraged to go through this discernment stage, paying close attention to what gave her consolation versus desolation, it became clear that she really was not interested in going right into the family business following her college graduation. She felt that going to work with her parents and brother would be infantilizing as she has always been the youngest and the only girl in the family and she felt that she was not treated as respectfully as she felt that she deserved. While acknowledging that she loved and admired her family, she admitted that she did not want to work with them around the clock for the near future and thus become enmeshed with them, both personally and professionally. Thus, the prospect of working in her family business gave her desolation rather than consolation. However, when she began to reflect on what she could do with her art talents, she found some consolation. She was lost in and excited by her art interests and by a friend of hers who had found her way into the fashion industry in New York City, creating artwork for fashion shows. She remained in close contact with her friend, visited her a few times in New York, and felt excited and energized by the prospect of following her friend's path into the fashion world. Her friend offered to help her do so and even invited her to live with her and her roommates if she moved to New York.

Rod, in the case example above, was also encouraged to reflect on what gave him consolation versus desolation. His efforts led him to conclude that continuing to work for a boss and company that he found "sleazy" was not a good option or fit for him. He had several friends and acquaintances who were working in nonprofit agencies that focus on conservation, climate change issues, and ecology. He reported that he always enjoyed listening to their stories and observations when they got together for social events. Reflecting on working for these nonprofits energized and activated his interests, and he decided to speak to his friends and their suggested referral sources for more information about possible job prospects and opportunities. He knew that if he moved from his current position, he would take a significant salary cut that would affect his family and his lifestyle, and so he decided to call a family meeting to discuss his thinking with his wife and children.

Jen and Rob's reflections and attention to consolation and desolation resulted in some worries that they would be rejected or receive significant push back from important people in their lives. Therefore, time was needed in therapy to discuss and reflect on what might happen to these relationships as well as strategies for communicating their true desires to important family members.

Exercise 4.4 Consolation vs. Desolation

As you reflect on what you have learned in the previous exercises in this chapter, think about five things, decisions, and pathways that give you consolation. Write them down here.

Consolation

1. _____

2. _____

3. _____

4. _____

5. _____

Now, reflect on five things, decisions, and pathways that give you desolation. Write them down here.

Desolation

1. _____

2. _____

3. _____

4. _____

5. _____

What has this exercise taught you? What reflections do you have now?

_____

_____

_____

_____

_____

Direction

The last step in the discernment process focuses on direction, next steps, and a path forward. The direction phase might include only a small next step or a next phase in life, and thus the process of the four Ds must be considered in an ongoing manner and not something that is entertained or conducted just once (Plante, 2017, 2019).

In the case of Jen and Rod, both decided to have heart-to-heart talks with their families to inform them of their desire to change their life plans. Jen's parents were not happy with her news but agreed to let her try her hand in the art world under certain circumstances. Rod's wife and children were supportive of his efforts to make a career move and accepted that his income would be lower in doing so and that their lifestyle might change in the near future.

Once Jen and Rod moved forward with their plans, they understood that ongoing reflection and discernment using the four Ds was necessary to continue to make good decisions in their lives.

Exercise 4.5 Finding Direction

After completing the earlier exercises in this chapter, do you have a sense of direction for your next steps in your life? What are your options? Write them down. Then list the pros and cons for each one.

Your Options	Pros	Cons
1.		
2.		
3.		
4.		
5.		
6.		
7.		
8.		
9.		
10.		

What does this exercise suggest to you? Are there changes in your life you wish to consider now?

_____

_____

_____

_____

_____

_____

Strategies to Include and Nurture the Four *D*s in Your Life

There are several principles to keep in mind to nurture the four *D*s in your life. These include using the four *D*s often and not being concerned about making errors in the discernment process as it is all part of the process in reflective and thoughtful decision making.

1. Use the Four *D*s Regularly

Once introduced and practiced, the four *D*s can be used daily to assist in decision making. It is a helpful strategy for both big and consequential decisions but also for smaller and less consequential decisions.

Case Example 4.3 Katie

Katie just graduated from college and is a bit immobilized and confused about what to do next with her life. She was a computer science major and ran on the track team throughout her college years. Her life has been so structured by both academics and track that she did not have much say in many of her day-to-day activities but rather just followed what was required of her by her academic and athletic goals. After graduation, she felt lost. She was not sure where she wanted to live or work and now that her track career was over, she had more time on her hands than felt comfortable.

Katie was introduced to the four *D*s and encouraged to use them on an ongoing and even daily basis to help her find direction and make decisions. They provided her with a decision-making process and structure that felt comfortable for her. In doing so, she found herself in a computer science internship program and then moved to another state to enjoy the discovery and adventure of a different style of living that was simpler and at a lower cost too. She worked at a media agency that was low-key, utilized her computer skills, and was in a lovely area that suited her sensibilities, at least for now.

Case Example 4.4 Carlos

Carlos was fired from his job following a conflict with his boss and a customer at his company. Carlos reported that he always had a short fuse and got angry quickly and easily, especially when he was frustrated. He admitted that he has trouble making decisions and that his frustration about his indecisive style often sets him up for an angry outburst. Carlos was introduced to the four *D*s as a process and structure for decision making and was encouraged to use this approach with decisions both large and small. He found the structure of the four *D*s helpful and provided him with a path through indecision that he never had before.

Exercise 4.6 Finding a Way to Regularly Reflect Using the 4 Ds

New habits are hard to do and make last. How can you incorporate the 4 Ds into your life on a regular basis? Could you take some time at the end or beginning of the day or week to spend 15 minutes or so reflecting on the 4 Ds in your life? Could you engage in conversations with loved ones about using the 4 Ds regularly in your lives? Is there a way for you to structure this reflection process into your regular life? How can you do it? What obstacles might get in the way?

Your Plans	Obstacles

1. _____

2. _____

3. _____

4. _____

5. _____

6. _____

7. _____

8. _____

9. _____

10. _____

2. Do Not Be Afraid to Make an Error in Discernment Decisions

The four Ds are no guarantee that all decisions using this approach will result in a good and satisfying outcome. Certainly, poor decisions may occur using this method, or any method, and there might be times when in retrospect, the four D process resulted in regrettable decisions (e.g., Doherty et al., 2016). This is yet another reason why using the four D approach should be an ongoing and regular exercise since if it contributes to a dead end or bad decision, clients can use the approach to get out of their poor or unhelpful decision and move towards a more satisfying one.

Case Example 4.5 Yasser

Yasser decided to use the four *D* approach to decide where to go for graduate school. The approach led him to decide to enter a PhD program in the sciences, but after two years he decided that he did not want to pursue an academic career and he did not like his major professor or her lab since everyone seemed unhappy and the workload was endless. Continuing to use the four *D*s, he decided to pivot and left the program after obtaining his master's degree seeking to work in industry. Yasser found this transition stressful but satisfying and was grateful to be moving on with his life rather than languishing in a doctoral program that he felt did not fit his career plans or desires.

Yasser used the four *D*s to make an important career decision to enter a doctoral program that ultimately proved to be a less satisfying decision. He pivoted using the four *D*s to change his plans leaving graduate school after his master's degree. Although his initial decision proved to be a mistake, he used the structure and process of the four *D*s to find a more suitable life path.

Case Example 4.6 Sal

Sal was conflicted about taking a job in another state. He was born and raised in New England and had a tempting job offer to relocate to Arizona for a position that paid more and seemed like a good fit for his skills and interest. He used the four *D*s to discern his options and ultimately decided to make the move to Arizona. However, once he arrived and settled there, he found that the climate was challenging for him, especially the summer heat, which reached 120 degrees and more on a regular basis. Additionally, his boss in Arizona proved to be difficult to work with, and some of the promises that were made before he accepted the job were not kept once he arrived there to start work. Finally, he found that he missed his New England roots, traditions, and both friends and family there. Going through the discernment process again, he decided to move back to New England after being in Arizona for about two years. He later felt that the experience provided growth for him but admits that he made a mistake in his discernment process in deciding to move there.

Exercise 4.7 Making Mistakes

Even with best intentions, we all make mistakes. What mistakes have you made in your life thus far? Write down the top five mistakes. If you had to do it all over again, what would you do differently?

Your Mistakes   **Do Differently?**

1. _____

2. _____

3. _____

4. _____

5. _____

Now, using the 4 *D*s, how might your decision making have altered these mistakes? Would they?

_____

_____

_____

What have you learned from this reflection?

_____

_____

_____

_____

Conclusion

The four *D*s are a useful and productive structure and process to make both big and small decisions. While this discernment process comes from Ignatian spirituality and the Jesuits, it can be easily adapted and used in both spiritual and secular environments (Liebert, 2008; Plante, 2017, 2020). People generally find that the four *D*s are very helpful to them and after minimal introduction and some training, they can be used by almost anyone at any time. The four *D*s can be used on an ongoing basis and even daily to find a path that leads to better decision making, providing direction with consolation rather than desolation. For those who are spiritually and religiously focused, the four *D*s can be used to assist in finding the divine's will or calling as well.

Further Reading

Dougherty, R. M. (2009). *Discernment: A path to spiritual awakening.* Paulist Press.

Liebert, E. (2008). *The way of discernment: Spiritual practices for decision making.* Westminster John Knox Press.

Plante, T. G. (2017). The 4 Ds: Using Ignatian spirituality in secular psychotherapy and beyond. *Spirituality in Clinical Practice, 4*(1), 74–79.

References

Bishop, J., & Carlton, R. (2016). Thomas Aquinas, SJ: A Thomistic analysis of Ignatian consolation and desolation. *Toronto Journal of Theology, 32*(1), 113–124.

Buckley, M. J. (1973). The structure of the rules for discernment of spirits. *The Way, 20,* 19–37.

Crusius, J., Corcoran, K., & Mussweiler, T. (2022). Social comparison: Theory, research, and applications. In D. Chadee, *Theories in social psychology* (2nd ed.; pp. 165–187). Wiley Blackwell.

Doherty, W. J., Harris, S. M., & Wilde, J. L. (2016). Discernment counseling for "mixed-agenda" couples. *Journal of Marital and Family Therapy, 42*(2), 246–255.

Dougherty, R. M. (2009). *Discernment: A path to spiritual awakening.* Paulist Press.

Futrell, J. C. (1970). Ignatian discernment. *Studies in the Spirituality of Jesuits, 2*(2), 47–88.

Gula, R. M. (1997). *Moral discernment.* Paulist Press.

Liebert, E. (2008). *The way of discernment: Spiritual practices for decision making.* Westminster John Knox Press.

Lienhard, J. T. (1980). On "discernment of spirits" in the early church. *Theological Studies, 41*(3), 505–529.

Nancy, J.-L. (2006). Consolation, desolation. *Epoché: A Journal for the History of Philosophy, 10*(2), 197–202.

Plante, T. G. (2017). The 4 Ds: Using Ignatian spirituality in secular psychotherapy and beyond. *Spirituality in Clinical Practice, 4*(1), 74–79.

Plante, T. G. (2020). St. Ignatius as psychotherapist?: How Jesuit spirituality and wisdom can enhance psychotherapy. *Spirituality in Clinical Practice, 7*(1), 65–71.

Suls, J., & Wheeler, L. (Eds.). (2013). *Handbook of social comparison: Theory and research.* Springer Science & Business Media.

Suls, J. E., & Wills, T. A. E. (1991). *Social comparison: Contemporary theory and research.* Lawrence Erlbaum Associates, Inc.

CHAPTER 5

Daily Reflection Using the Examen

In the last chapter, the four *D*s of discernment and decision making were featured, highlighting a structured, organized, and step-by-step pathway for making thoughtful and good decisions. Another tool in the Jesuit spirituality toolbox that can also assist in the reflection and discernment process is the Examen. The Examen is an end-of-the-day, five-step reflective prayer that reviews the day in a structured, systematic, and thoughtful manner and plans for the next day to come (Manney, 2011). It is a common and popular tool among those interested in and engaged by Jesuit-inspired spirituality and can be altered in ways that can easily appeal to a diverse audience of both religious and nonreligious persons. Like other spiritually and religiously based approaches, such as mindfulness and yoga, the Examen can be adapted in a variety of ways to be fully embraced by those who have no interest in spirituality and religion. In this chapter, I will outline and detail the Examen and provide examples that are both secular as well as religiously based. In this way, readers can get a sense of how the Examen was originally constructed and used within a religious context yet also see how it can be adapted in a completely secular manner. In general, the Examen is flexible and adaptable. Those who use the Examen may wish to follow the order of the steps that were suggested by St. Ignatius and the Jesuits so many years ago, but they may wish to edit the details in a way that is useful for their intended purposes or for the individual who may or may not be open to religious or spiritual language and approaches.

The Examen includes five steps that are typically completed within about 15 minutes. The first step of the Examen is to put oneself in God's (or the sacred as understood by the participant) presence. The second step encourages one to give thanks and to be grateful for various points and experiences in one's day thus far. The third step reviews the experiences of the current day reflecting on what went well and what went poorly while focusing on the presence of the divine or sacred during the key moments and inflection points throughout the day. The fourth step encourages a reflection on one's challenges and shortcomings looking for potential improvements in thought and behavior that might be attempted and committed to moving forward later in the day and tomorrow. The final step includes planning and looking forward to the next day while reflecting upon what one learned from the careful review of the current day.

Table 5.1 provides the list of Examen steps from both a spiritual/religious perspective and from a secular perspective. While either approach may be helpful and can be used as desired, the five-step process should not be altered in order to keep the approach consistent with the wisdom, spirit, and tradition of the Examen.

TABLE 5.1 Five Steps of the Examen: Religious and Secular

Religious	Secular
1. Put self in God's presence	1. Quiet and center the mind with silence
2. Give thanks to God	2. Be grateful
3. Review the day attending to God's presence	3. Review the day's good moments
4. Attend to daily shortcomings	4. Attend to daily shortcomings
5. Invite God to be with you tomorrow	5. Plan for tomorrow and to do better

While the Examen is popular among Christians, and most especially those who are influenced by Jesuit spirituality, it could easily be adapted to accommodate the interests and values of a religiously diverse, including a completely secular, audience (Plante, 1999, 2009, 2017). St. Ignatius and the Jesuits have encouraged the use of the Examen by diverse audiences including both religious and nonreligious communities (Chinnici, 1997; Martin, 2021; Tetlow, 1994). Therefore, efforts to secularize the Examen are not new but have been encouraged for many years and even centuries. The Examen has also been used as a cognitive behavioral style intervention or tool in various types of mental health treatment and care (Plante, 2021), including couples therapy (e.g., Priester, 2006) and worker burnout (e.g., Case et al., 2020; McMillin, 2021).

Let us take a closer look at the Examen and provide some examples, both religious and secular, of its use in clinical treatment. Tables 5.2 and 5.3 provide examples of the Examen from a religious (Table 5.2) and nonreligious or secular perspective (Table 5.3).

TABLE 5.2 A Sample Examen for Religious Audiences

> **IGNATIAN EXAMEN**
> **15 minutes of pause, reflection, and prayer together.**

Step 1: Place yourself in the presence of God, the divine, or the sacred

Let us put ourselves in the holy presence of God, asking God for the light to see His will and plan for us.

Let us take a big healing breath, focus our attention, and push aside our many distractions.

Step 2: Gratitude

What are you grateful for today? Consider big gratitude examples like your life, love, family, and health, as well as little ones like a good sleep, a cup of coffee, or a bite of chocolate.

Spend a moment giving thanks and praise to God for the gifts that you have received from His divine graciousness and many blessings.

Step 3: A review of the day

Going moment by moment, review your day. In your imagination, relive each significant moment of the day thus far. Linger at the important moments and pass quickly through the less relevant ones. Continue expressing gratitude to God for the day lived so far and the many blessings received.

Step 4: Face your challenges, shortcomings, and sins

Reflect on the difficult moments of your day—when you had unhelpful thought patterns, impulses, sins, and temptations. Reflect on what you said or did that was hurtful, or when you were hurt. Pay attention to any missed opportunities for graciousness, compassion, and love. Consider if there is an invitation to healing, forgiveness, or reconciliation. Pray for grace and forgiveness.

Allow God's divine mercy and love to be absorbed into your being.

IGNATIAN EXAMEN 15 minutes of pause, reflection, and prayer together.

Step 5: Planning for tomorrow and next steps

Given your reflection and prayer today, what are you invited to do for the rest of today and for tomorrow? What sort of person are you called to be now? Resolve to be that person. Pray and ask God's help to assist you in fulfilling your commitment.

Conclude:

Take another deep healing breath and end in your usual way.

Are there any final things you want to express?

Is there a prayer or intention you want to say?

Amen.

TABLE 5.3 A Sample Examen for More Diverse and Secular Audiences

IGNATIAN EXAMEN 15 minutes of pause and reflection together.

Step 1: Place yourself in a calm and relaxed position

Prepare: Begin in your usual way.

Let us take a big healing breath, focus our attention, and push aside our many distractions.

Step 2: Gratitude

What are you grateful for today? Consider big gratitude examples like your life, love, family, and health, as well as little ones as well like a good sleep, a cup of coffee, or a bite of chocolate.

Spend a moment appreciating the advantages and gifts you have received.

Step 3: Review your day

Going moment by moment, review the day. In your imagination, relive each significant moment of the day thus far. Linger at the important moments and pass quickly through the less relevant ones. Continue expressing gratitude for the day lived so far.

Step 4: Face your challenges and shortcomings

Reflect on the difficult moments of the day—when you had unhelpful thought patterns, when you said or did something hurtful, or when you were hurt. Pay attention to any missed opportunities for graciousness, compassion, and love. Consider if there is an invitation to healing, forgiveness, or reconciliation.

Step 5: Planning for tomorrow and next steps

Given your reflection today, what are you invited to do for the rest of today and for tomorrow? What sort of person are you called to be now? Resolve to be that person.

Conclude:

Take another deep healing breath and end in your usual way.

Are there any final things you want to express?

Is there an intention you want to say?

The Five Steps of the Examen

Step 1: Place Yourself in the Presence of God, the Divine, or the Sacred

We are often extremely busy and distracted by our many issues of the day and the practicalities of life. We sometimes refer to this situation as having "monkey brain," referring to our highly distractible way of being in our fast-paced contemporary society (Oye, 2014). It is challenging for most people to stop and put aside all the diverse demands on our attention, even for just a few minutes. We are so used to multiple inputs coming from multiple directions, including our computers and smartphones, the people at home and work who surround us, constant breaking news, and our own internal chatter. We tend to lose our ability to focus our attention and turn off the cacophony of sounds, demands, and distractions that surround us (Strayer & Cooper, 2015). Step one of the Examen seeks to put ourselves into a quiet, peaceful, reflective, and perhaps prayerful space that pushes aside all the distractions that request or demand our attention. Since the Examen process is only expected to last 15 minutes, step one is not a heavy lift or too onerous to accomplish for most people.

Most meditative, contemplative, and prayer practices across the various spiritual and religious traditions request that we stop everything and focus our attention on a particular task or stimulus. Different religious, spiritual, and secular traditions have different ways to do this with some requesting that we sit quietly in a meditative posture (e.g., the lotus position) or focus our attention on our breath, a candle, a religious or spiritual icon or statue, or other ways to assist in our focus (Plante, 2010). When using the process of the Examen, there is a call or a directive to place oneself in the presence of God or the divine. This can be accomplished in multiple ways depending on one's religious or spiritual beliefs, traditions, and individual desires. It essentially suggests that we tune out our many distractions and sit, kneel, or stand in a quiet place and do whatever we need to do to place ourselves in the presence of the divine or the sacred, as we understand these concepts. This might include gazing at a statue, a painting, or a photo or perhaps just sitting quietly with our eyes closed. A variety of meditative, contemplative, and prayerful traditions and approaches, including the Examen, also might suggest taking a deep breath that can help relax, organize, and center us. Perhaps a religious and a secular example may prove useful.

Religious Case Example 5.1 Luz

Luz is in her 30s and immigrated to the United States from Colombia. She found a position at a Spanish-speaking news outlet. Most of her family and friends remain in Colombia, and she is struggling with the transition to the United States, which includes living in a different culture with different values and expectations. Luz considers herself deeply spiritual and religious and is disappointed by the secular nature of her new life and community. In recent months, she has developed anxiety and depressive symptoms and sought assistance from her Employee Assistance Program at work. In addition to standard cognitive behavioral therapy and cultural humility, her therapist suggested using the Examen. Luz readily agreed to use the Examen in addition to the other suggestions her therapist offered.

Luz reported that she always has had a special devotion to Mary, the mother of Jesus, and the iconic image of Our Lady of Guadalupe (see Poole, 2017). In the image, Mary is surrounded by roses, and Luz reports that she loves the smell of roses. Luz decided to use the image of Our Lady of Guadalupe that she has framed in her apartment and an actual fragrant rose next to the picture when possible. She uses this image, and scent, to help her place herself in the presence of the divine, taking a deep breath to begin her Examen process.

Secular Case Example 5.2 Raj

Raj is from India and moved to the United States for a job in the technology industry. Although he grew up within the Hindu tradition, he experiences himself now as secular and not especially interested in religion or spirituality. Raj finds that religion can be oppressive and that his more scientific background led him to become an agnostic. Raj does enjoy nature and hiking in the nearby mountains. He finds peace, solace, and the sacred in nature. He loves the high Sierra of California in particular. He has enjoyed hiking with friends as well as with the Sierra Club during periodic vacations and long weekends.

Raj feels that he can sometimes be "a jerk" at work. His relationships with some coworkers are often strained, and he has ruffled some feathers in his interactions with many of his colleagues. He admits that he can be short with people and that he can ignore the feelings of others depending more on rationality and evidence rather than emotions and personal relationships. He justifies his actions by stating that to stay competitive in the technology field, one must be driven and demand success and top performance from everyone. He uses such high-profile visionary technology leaders as Steve Jobs, Larry Ellison, and Elon Musk as his role models. However, he agreed that his style does not always achieve his goals and that he should work on his relationship skills. He entered therapy after his wife divorced him. He was open to trying a secular version of the Examen when his therapist suggested it.

Raj uses an image of Mount Whitney, the highest point in the continental United States, as a comforting image to help center himself as step one of the Examen. He takes a deep breath and visualizes Mount Whitney, a majestic and sacred spot in his mind, to begin the Examen process.

Once we place ourselves in the presence of the divine or sacred, in whatever way that feels comfortable and meaningful to us, we are ready for the second step of the Examen, which focuses on gratitude.

Step 2: Gratitude

The second step of the Examen is reflecting on gratitude. It suggests that we reflect on the various aspects of our day and life for which we are grateful. This might include big and substantial elements like the gift of life, our families, our health, our home, and so forth. It also includes acknowledging our gratitude for the smaller things that we are grateful for, such as a good cup of coffee, a sunny day, a delicious bite of chocolate, or a kind gesture by a colleague, friend, family member, or even a stranger. The practice of gratitude has been demonstrated in multiple research studies to be a helpful way to cope better with negative affect and enhance mood, efficacy, and better coping as well (Emmons & Stern, 2013; Jans-Beken et al., 2020; Worthen & Isakson, 2007).

Religious Case Example 5.1 Luz

Luz reflects on what she is grateful for, and she is pleased that she has a job that pays pretty well, and she is grateful for the love of her family and friends. She also expresses gratitude for her faith and for the Church that she attends. She admits that her life is a great gift to her and believes that God provides her with many blessings each day. Luz is also grateful that she is a good cook who can make herself and loved ones tasty meals.

Secular Case Example 5.2 Raj

Raj is also grateful for his job and life. He expresses gratitude for living close enough to many compelling nature locations that are accessible to him. He also expresses gratitude that he has a reverse commute each day and thus, unlike many of his colleagues, his daily ritual of getting to and from work is usually smooth. Raj also expresses gratitude that his health is good and that he is athletic enough to go on hikes when he has the time to do so. He is also grateful for the pleasure of a sporting event he is about to enjoy watching on TV.

Once we review the aspects of our life and day that we are grateful for in a thoughtful and reflective manner, we are ready for the third step of the Examen, a careful review of the day.

Step 3: A Review of the Day

The third step of the Examen is to review the various moments of the day and give thanks for the parts that went well, yet seeking to better understand or appreciate the parts that did not go as well. Reviewing the day, hour by hour or moment by moment, is recommended during this Examen step. We are then asked to see where the divine or the sacred was present during each of these moments and how we were blessed or graced during those important inflection points and experiences. This review process includes a careful accounting of the day and efforts to try to learn how the day unfolded and how God (or the divine and sacred) was found or not found during these various inflection points and moments.

Religious Case Example 5.1 Luz

Luz believes that the divine and Jesus, in particular, live within us all. As Luz reviews her day, she noted how she interacted with a child on the subway that was connecting and fun. She noted how Jesus did not turn children away when they approached him and noted how important they are (Matthew 18). She tried to do the same with her interaction with the child on the subway. Additionally, she noted how she picked up the hat of an elderly woman who dropped it on the street while Luz was walking to work. Luz fondly remembers the smile and thank-you that the stranger offered her. Luz also recalled the frustration she experienced working with her boss earlier in the day who was pressuring her to meet an unrealistic deadline. Luz noted the laugh she shared with a coworker while riding in the elevator and enjoyed the brief interaction with her. Luz attended noon mass at a parish a few blocks away during her lunch break and remembered the homily of the priest that gave her something important to think about after lunch. Luz also recalled being tired at the end of the day and turning on the news, feeling upset and disappointed with the difficult situations and pain experienced by so many people highlighted in the newscast.

Secular Case Example 5.2 Raj

Raj reviewed his day and was grateful that his commute was easy and that the coffee at work was delicious. He expressed gratitude for a business deal that looked promising and likely to close earlier than expected. However, he also noted that he felt upset after hearing a report about how climate change would negatively affect his beloved mountains in the high Sierra. He fretted about the lack of snow, the risks of wildfire, and the recession of an important glacier. Raj reflected that people do not respect the importance and sacredness of nature as much as they should. Raj noted several interactions with coworkers during the day where he tried to be friendlier but felt that his gestures were not appreciated or acknowledged. Raj noted how he was a bit cranky with someone on his way home when he stopped to do an errand. He admitted that he felt bad about the interaction, stating that he could have been better behaved.

Once the day is reviewed carefully and thoughtfully, one is ready to move to step four, facing our challenges and shortcomings.

Step 4: Facing Challenges and Shortcomings

The fourth step of the Examen encourages us to face our challenges and shortcomings. As we review the day, there may have been moments and experiences where we were not at our best. Perhaps we were rude, selfish, overly angry or irritable with others, and so forth. This step of the Examen, perhaps the most difficult and challenging for most people, suggests that we look for our failures or for those moments when we did not act in accordance with our values or our preferred and idealized image of ourselves. This stage invites us to remember our values and goals and to make a commitment to address and incorporate them moving forward. This stage of the Examen can even be painful for some people since it requires that we focus on failures, weaknesses, and failings that may have deeply hurt and affected others. This stage can result in depressive feelings or despair. However, we are encouraged to remind ourselves that no one is perfect and to be honest with ourselves, we must acknowledge our many failings. This stage provides some fresh, honest, and hopefully helpful information to move into the final stage of the Examen, planning for tomorrow.

Religious Case Example 5.1 Luz

As Luz completes the fourth stage of the Examen, she gets in touch with the high expectations she holds for herself and others, as well as her selfishness at times. She admits that she often tries to be good to earn a place in heaven or achieve the praise of others. She reminds herself of the homily message at mass earlier in the day about not showing off your piousness like the religious leaders of the day did during Jesus's time but rather praying, fasting, and working privately so as not to draw attention to our good deeds. This Gospel message (Matthew 6) hit home for her, and she recommitted to trying to act on it more thoughtfully and with intention. Luz also got in touch with her sassy side when she complained about her boss to several of her coworkers. She admits that some of her comments might have been ungenerous and could lead to work rumors. She commits to being more gracious moving forward. She prays that God will grant her the strength to be better and acknowledges that as St. Paul states in his letter to the Romans (3:23), "All have sinned and fallen short of the glory of God."

Secular Case Example 5.2 Raj

During stage four of the Examen, Raj reflects that he can be an "asshole" at times, especially with his subordinates and some coworkers. He admits that he can be bossy and that his lack of generosity and understanding can be off-putting with people at work. He notes that he is much calmer and more peaceful when he is in nature and wonders how he might translate that quality into his work environment. He commits to hanging nature photos in his office to help him reflect on his behavior and feel the calming influence of the outdoors. He also ponders asking his coworkers and subordinates for forgiveness or at least acknowledge to them that he has been unkind and will strive to do better.

After an honest, open, and careful assessment of challenges and shortcomings, we are ready for the final stage of the Examen, planning for tomorrow.

Step 5: Planning for Tomorrow

The insights provided from stage four then set the stage for planning for tomorrow. The Examen process suggests that we can plan to be better in our interactions and activities from the knowledge that we have learned about ourselves today during the 15-minute Examen process. Stage five of the Examen suggests developing a working action plan to move in a better and more productive life-giving direction for tomorrow. Stage five of the Examen suggests that we actively and intentionally work on our challenges and shortcomings, trying our best to make progress in these important and often difficult areas of growth. This might include living one's values more or trying to be better at relationships or activities.

Religious Case Example 5.1 Luz

Luz resolves to be more selfless and generous in her actions. She decided to use a Gospel quote from the homily that she heard at mass today (i.e., Matthew 6:1—"Be careful not to practice your righteousness in front of others to be seen by them. If you do, you will have no reward from your Father in heaven") and tape it on her refrigerator to remind her of her need to be humbler. She also decided that she will recite the Jesus Prayer (i.e., "Lord Jesus Christ, have mercy on me, a sinner") when she confronts challenging situations and experiences tomorrow as well.

Secular Case Example 5.2 Raj

Raj decided to develop a plan to apologize to several of his coworkers and subordinates tomorrow. He decided that he will ask for their forgiveness and hope that reconciliation is possible in due time. He will acknowledge his faults and mention that he hopes to do better over time, knowing that it might occur in fits and starts as behavior is so difficult to change.

The Examen may end with an "Amen" or some gesture to finish the process and return to our regular activities. The Examen suggests that we engage in this process each day, perhaps at the end of the day before bed. The five steps take only about 15 minutes and so it can be easily accomplished, even for busy people. Additionally, it can be adapted in multiple ways so that it can appeal to many different types of people regardless of their interests or affiliations with spiritual or religious traditions, beliefs, and practices.

Exercise 5.1 Practice the Examen

Now that you have learned about the Examen and have seen how it can be used in both religious and secular ways, try it yourself. Use the tables at the end of this chapter to guide you in doing so. After you have tried it, what are your reflections? Write them here.

_____

_____

_____

Do you think you can try to use the Examen daily for a week and see how it works for you? Why or why not?

_____

_____

_____

Conclusion

The Examen is a daily cognitive process seeking to identify our challenging and unhealthy thoughts, emotions, and behaviors and then finding ways to alter them in a more healthy and productive direction. It also seeks to develop strategies to improve our thoughts and behaviors through cognitive restructuring, goal setting, and emphasis on gratitude, optimism, and so forth (Craske, 2010). The Examen is consistent with cognitive behavioral strategies and techniques.

To get the most benefit from the Examen experience, it should be practiced every day and, ideally, at the end of each day. You may wish to integrate the Examen into your typical end-of-day or bedtime routine and activities. In this way, you can depend on the Examen to help you better and productively reflect on your day while preparing for the day to come. Certainly, more research on the Examen, including randomized clinical trials, is needed, and hopefully it will be conducted and published in coming years. In the meantime, the Examen is a useful tool that takes only 15 minutes or so to complete and can be practiced in a variety of ways that can accommodate the needs, traditions, and desires of diverse people who are attracted to both religious and secular approaches.

Further Reading

Manney, J. (2011). *A simple, life-changing prayer: Discovering the power of St. Ignatius Loyola's Examen.* Loyola Press.

McMillin, S. E. (2021). Innovating vocational resilience: Getting a second start at work through the Ignatian Examen. *Social Work & Christianity, 48*(1), 5–9.

Plante, T. G. (2021). Using the Examen, a Jesuit prayer, in spiritually integrated and secular psychotherapy. *Pastoral Psychology, 71,* 119–125.

Tetlow, J. A. (1994). The most postmodern prayer: American Jesuit identity and the Examen of conscience, 1920–1990. *Studies in the Spirituality of Jesuits, 26*(1), 1–92.

References

Case, A. D., Keyes, C. L. M., Huffman, K. F., Sittser, K., Wallace, A., Khatiwoda, P., Parnell, H. E., & Proeschold-Bell, R. J. (2020). Attitudes and behaviors that differentiate clergy with positive mental health from those with burnout. *Journal of Prevention & Intervention in the Community, 48*(1), 94–112.

Chinnici, J. P. (1997). Culture and prayer: Towards a history of contemplation in the Catholic community in the United States. *U.S. Catholic Historian, 15*(4), 1–16.

Craske, M. G. (2010). *Cognitive-behavioral therapy.* American Psychological Association.

Emmons, R. A., & Stern, R. (2013). Gratitude as a psychotherapeutic intervention. *Journal of Clinical Psychology, 69*(8), 846–855.

Jans-Beken, L., Jacobs, N., Janssens, M., Peeters, S., Reijnders, J., Lechner, L., & Lataster, J. (2020). Gratitude and health: An updated review. *Journal of Positive Psychology, 15*(6), 743–782.

Manney, J. (2011). *A simple, life-changing prayer: Discovering the power of St. Ignatius Loyola's Examen.* Loyola Press.

Martin, J. (2021). *Learning to pray: A guide for everyone.* HarperOne.

McMillin, S. E. (2021). Innovating vocational resilience: Getting a second start at work through the Ignatian Examen. *Social Work & Christianity, 48*(1), 5–9.

Oye, J. (2014). *Monkeybrain: Create emotional balance, physical health, and spiritual awareness: Brain-body-spirit, the practical approach.* Balboa Press.

Plante, T. G. (1999). A collaborative relationship between professional psychology and the Roman Catholic Church: A case example and suggested principles for success. *Professional Psychology: Research and Practice, 30*(6), 541–546.

Plante, T. G. (2009). *Spiritual practices in psychotherapy: Thirteen tools for enhancing psychological health.* American Psychological Association.

Plante, T. G. (Ed). (2010). *Contemplative practices in action: Spirituality, meditation, and health.* Praeger/ABC-CLIO.

Plante, T. G. (2017). The 4 Ds: Using Ignatian spirituality in secular psychotherapy and beyond. *Spirituality in Clinical Practice, 4*(1), 74–79.

Plante, T. G. (2021). Using the Examen, a Jesuit prayer, in spiritually integrated and secular psychotherapy. *Pastoral Psychology, 71,* 119–125.

Poole, S. (2017). *Our Lady of Guadalupe: The origins and sources of a Mexican national symbol, 1531–1797.* University of Arizona Press.

Priester, P. E. (2006). Integrating the discernment of spiritual guidance in family and couples therapy: Use of the examen. In K. B. Helmeke & C. Ford Sori (eds.), *The therapist's notebook for integrating spirituality in counseling: Homework, handouts, and activities for use in psychotherapy* (pp. 287–292). Routledge.

Strayer, D. L., & Cooper, J. M. (2015). Driven to distraction. *Human factors, 57*(8), 1343–1347.

Tetlow, J. A. (1994). The most postmodern prayer: American Jesuit Identity and the Examen of conscience, 1920–1990. *Studies in the Spirituality of Jesuits, 26*(1), 1–92.

Worthen, V. E., & Isakson, R. L. (2007). The therapeutic value of experiencing and expressing gratitude. *Issues in Religion and Psychotherapy, 31*(1), 5.

CHAPTER 6

Managing Conflict with Accommodation, Humility, and the Expectation of Goodness

People and groups have always experienced interpersonal and intergroup conflict that has too often escalated into hate, cruelty, oppression, violence, and warfare. Perhaps since the dawn of time, people have had difficulty getting along with each other. Sadly, many people have been both victimized and traumatized by important people in their lives. Even more tragically, many people have been victimized by those with whom they are closest to and trust the most. These often include spouses, children, parents, and other family members.

During recent years, interpersonal and intergroup conflicts have appeared to get much worse with increased divisiveness, hate, taunting cruelty, oppression, and vitriol (Bilewicz & Soral, 2020; Fischer et al., 2018; Piazza, 2020). Social media makes these problems much worse since everyone now has a bullhorn to spread hate across the globe (Sheth et al., 2022). It appears that many people enjoy and take great satisfaction in insulting, canceling, and correcting others with whom they disagree or dislike. With an internet connection and a social media platform, anyone can say anything about anybody. The more outrageous and horrific the attack, the more attention people seem to get, thereby reinforcing and encouraging their hateful behavior (Arthur, 2021).

Many people experience challenges with difficult interpersonal relationships and challenging conflicts with family members, coworkers, and others. They are often devastated and distraught about how these important and previously trusting relationships have soured and experience a range of emotions about these various important people in their lives. Tragically, many of these conflicts lead to depression, alienation, desperation, and even suicide. Thus, managing conflicts with others and problem solving these conflictual relationships are a critically important topic.

Jesuit spirituality and tradition offer an insightful and helpful three-step process that can be an important and valuable tool in managing conflict between individuals and between groups. Building on several of the principles discussed earlier in this book (e.g., seeing the sacred in all, reflection, and discernment), this three-step model can be applied to numerous and diverse interpersonal and intergroup situations where tensions and conflicts exist and escalate. This three-step process can be used in a religiously or spiritually informed and embraced manner or in a completely secular approach as well. It involves (1) accommodation, (2) humility, and (3) the expectation of goodness.

St. Ignatius, founder of the Jesuits, stated that when there is conflict between people, one should "approach individuals with love and a desire for their well-being, while carefully observing each person's temperament and character" (O'Malley, 1993, p. 111). Furthermore, he advises that we should "be more eager to put a good interpretation on a neighbor's statement than to condemn it. Further, if one cannot interpret it favorably, one should ask how the other means it. If that meaning is wrong, one should correct the person with love; and if this is not enough, one should search out every appropriate means through which, by understanding the statement in a good way, it may be saved" (Spiritual Exercises, 31; no. 22; see Ignatius, 2000). St. Ignatius also suggests that we should be "be slow to speak (and) be considerate and kind ... considering the reasons on both sides ... giving your opinion with the greatest possible humility" (Ignatius, 2000). This sage advice from St. Ignatius from 500 years ago can be thoughtfully utilized and integrated into psychotherapy for clients who struggle with relationship troubles and conflicts.

Taken together, advice from St. Ignatius and contemporary Jesuit spirituality suggests that this three-step process of managing challenging relationships can be helpful and provides a useful structure and pathway for conflict resolution. Thus, when approaching people or groups in conflict, one should keep the following three concepts in mind: (1) accommodation (i.e., starting where the other person is), (2) humility (i.e., listen first and do not presume to know), and (3) expect goodness (i.e., use empathy and set aside one's ego focusing on the good in the person and what is emerging as you converse). Let me now unpack and provide examples of this three-step process for managing challenging and conflictual relationships and conversations.

Accommodation

It is often very difficult for us to understand others and the reasons why they think or behave as they do. People may have different political or religious points of view or seem much more liberal or conservative than we are. We may often think that the world and our communities would be much better off if everyone thought and acted just as we do. We may especially be put off by people who think and act in ways that are very different from our ways of doing things and perhaps among those who seem to have little tolerance for viewpoints different from their own.

Accommodation refers to trying to get into the mind and culture of others to understand their point of view and where their ideas and perspectives might be coming from. Accommodation seeks to better understand the lived experience of the person we disagree with or dislike. As St. Ignatius stated, it is starting the conversation where the other person is.

We naturally see people who we dislike or disagree with as "the other." We may believe that they are misguided, stupid, evil, corrupt, nasty, and so forth. We may find it easy to hate or demonize others. For example, perhaps one of the most vilified and hated groups of people in our society is pedophiles, who are adults who sexually violate children (Klein, 2015; Murray, 2000). When these sex offenders have positions of authority and trust with children and families, such as schoolteachers, coaches, tutors, or clerics, we get especially irate (Salter, 2018).

There are many groups of people in society whom many especially may despise and demonize. These groups include not only criminals (e.g., murderers, rapists) but also perhaps people in our own lives, such as a coworker, boss, relative, or neighbor. Sadly, some people despise their own spouse. There is a lot not to like in some people, and we may quickly learn to hate and demonize many whom we know well, casually, or just have read about in the press.

Accommodation seeks to get into their skin to try to understand their point of view or perspective. People are usually much more complex, with layers of influencing factors contributing to why they act as they do. One excellent and striking example of accommodation is an episode of the popular CNN television show *United Shades of America*, hosted by and starring W. Kamau Bell, a popular comedian who lives in the Berkeley, California, area (Bell, 2018). Bell is an exceedingly likable and open-minded African American man who featured the Ku Klux Klan (KKK) on one of his shows. He interviewed KKK members and their leaders for the show. His interviews focused on how to better understand what motivates them to do what they do and what factors contribute to their hateful prejudice and discrimination towards African Americans among other groups. In his typically humorous yet charming manner, he treats these KKK leaders and members with respect and dignity and asks them straightforward questions (such as where do they get the wood for their cross burnings) in an inquisitive and thoughtful manner. He tries to get into their heads. He seeks to understand their beliefs and practices, and in doing so, he disarms and charms them. Before you know it, the KKK members and leaders, notorious for their extreme discrimination and hate, especially towards those who are African American, are enjoying their time with Bell and treating him with great respect and dignity. He seems to have won them over, at least during the television show, in a way that, hopefully, lessens their hate and discrimination moving forward. Bell uses accommodation to start the conversation from where the KKK members are at and does so in a neutral, disarming, and respectful manner that helps to move the conversation forward productively, and in the show, rather entertainingly too.

It is much too easy to judge others from afar. We may make strong and harsh judgments about people we do not like or know without a fuller and more complete understanding of them or their backgrounds. It is easy to judge and reject others rather than seek to better understand them. Accommodation asks us to try to understand others in a more neutral manner without quick judgments and rejections.

Case Example 6.1 James

James is a nine-year-old boy who has already put two teachers in the hospital. He bit one in the leg so hard and for so long that she needed surgery to repair her leg. He also broke the nose of another teacher when she tried to constrain him during a classroom temper tantrum. James is so difficult to manage that an attendant—a large burly young man—accompanies him whenever he is at school or at other locations outside of his home.

Everyone who knew him, including his own family members, vilified James. James was an unwanted child from the start of his life. His mother became pregnant with him right before a bitter divorce and he represented to his biological parents the failed marriage that they ended shortly after he was born. The parents admitted that neither of them really wanted James when he was born, and they both had quickly moved on with other relationships, marriages, and children.

Although it was easy to dislike James given his extreme aggression and acting-out behavior, it was important to accommodate in trying to understand him from his perspective. He was a rejected child and absorbed the rejection from his parents and others, turning the difficult feelings into profound anger and a conduct disorder.

Case Example 6.2 Quintina

Quintina has four older brothers and is having difficulties and conflicts with several of them. Quintina leans left politically and is appalled by the very conservative and right-wing tendencies of several of her brothers. She is troubled and conflicted about what to do regarding upcoming end-of-the-year holidays where her family typically gathers to celebrate Christmas and News Year's together as a long-established family tradition. She is considering not attending these celebrations as her brothers love to talk politics and give her a hard time about her political and cultural views. Quintina's husband really does not want to attend the gatherings either but warns her that not attending would be a slap in the face to the family. Quintina is deeply distressed by these issues and has been losing sleep about her dilemma. She sought therapy to help her figure out how best to proceed.

Quintina was encouraged to try to accommodate to better understand her brothers' views by trying to appreciate where they were coming from. Her brothers are blue-collar workers who have struggled to make a living and feel that the political left has abandoned them and their concerns. They are appalled by liberal, "woke" culture and feel alienated from progressive current times. Quintina's brothers were channeling their anger and upset into their relationship and interactions with her given her differing political and cultural views. Quintina also achieved more education than her brothers, and they resent her successes compared with their own. The fact that she is the youngest in the family—often referred to as "the baby sister"—makes these tensions and conflicts even worse.

Exercise 6.1 How Can You Practice Accommodation in Your Life?

Think about the half dozen or so people in your life who you really do not like at all. You might wish to refer back to Exercise 3.4 in Chapter 3. Perhaps they include a coworker, family member, neighbor, or someone you have never met before but have heard a lot about them, such as a politician or a celebrity. List them. What is it about each one that bothers you so much? List these qualities next to each name.

Six people who you dislike the most   **Qualities you dislike about them**

1. _____

2. _____

3. _____

4. _____

5. _____

6. _____

Now close your eyes and try to get into their skin to see the world from their perspective. Can you imagine why they do what they do that bothers you so much? What is it about their history or experiences that might have led them to their way of being in the world and with you? Write down your observations.

_____

_____

_____

_____

_____

_____

Do you notice any themes emerging from this exercise? Are there certain characteristics that are common among the people on your list? Might these themes say something about you?

As you imagine being in the skin of those you most dislike, can you understand them better? You do not need to agree with them or like them, but can you better understand them and their perspective?

Humility

Arrogance, confidence, strong opinions, and narcissism seem to be commonplace in our culture, and these qualities are typically reinforced both intentionally as well as unintentionally (Campbell et al., 2010; Tyler, 2007). Politicians, CEOs, sport stars, celebrities, and other high-profile people often project an image of having all the answers and the confidence to express them (Furedi, 2010; Holmes & Redmond, 2012). They get a great deal of attention and seem to be rewarded for their highly confident viewpoints. They then become models for others and so we all might feel that we need to behave like them, acting and sounding confident with strong views. Sadly, the message might seem to suggest that humility is for losers (Chancellor & Lyubomirsky, 2013).

However, the second step of our three-step process for better relationships and conflict resolution is humility, perhaps a quality that has gone out of fashion in some circles during current times (Frame, 2007). Humility means that we listen to others before speaking our mind. It means that we approach others with the view that we do not have all the answers but that we have much to learn from others. It suggests that we avoid harsh and confident judgments, especially with little or incomplete information to go on (Van Tongeren et al., 2019; Weidman et al., 2018).

We are often very quick to judge, and judge harshly, the behavior of others, regardless of how well we know or understand them. Certainly, biblical scripture often warns against judging others (see Matthew 7:1–5; John 8:1–8; Luke 6:31–36) and yet we do so nonetheless (Stalnaker, 2008). Perhaps we cannot help ourselves. To understand and manage our world, we are hard-wired to make quick judgments (Fiske, 2000). We need to know if the person approaching us is a friend or foe, for example. Over the centuries, we needed to know if people were part of our tribe or not and if they would help or hurt us (Schaller et al., 2003). Although this tendency to judge and to judge quickly has some benefits in many often life-and-death situations, it results in many unintended consequences of discrimination, racism, xenophobia, and oppression of others. People are complicated, and we simply do not have all the answers about them to really understand them and their motives. Thus, we need to practice humility and acknowledge that we do not know everything or have all the information necessary to judge others.

This second step of humility suggests that as we approach others with whom we are in conflict, we should embrace the spirit of humility. The example provided earlier with W. Kamau Bell is an excellent example of this expression of humility. He approaches these KKK leaders with what appeared to be a sincere interest and with humility in trying to understand their point of view and their historically horrific behavior. He did not call them racists, monsters, or criminals but rather respectfully approached them as humans with ideas and behaviors that perplexed him. This humility offers an opportunity to understand others rather than simply picking sides and being overly defensive, or talking at each other rather than with each other. Humility sets the stage for an openness to discussion and conflict resolution rather than an escalation of conflict and digging in of one's heels trying to convince others of your viewpoints.

Case Example 6.1 James

Approaching James with humility meant trying not to overly judge or criticize him. His behavior certainly made those around him angry, disgusted, and rejecting, reinvading what he experienced from his parents and family members since his earliest days. James was referred to a child therapist who focused on trying to understand his perspective and behaviors as a human being and to help him develop more productive ways to respond to his distress.

Case Example 6.2 Quintina

Politics and the many societal challenges of the times are complicated with few simple and straightforward solutions. Quintina was encouraged to approach her brothers with humility and the fact that no one has all the answers or the expertise to solve so many complicated problems. She was encouraged to talk with her brothers about their views in ways that would be understandable to those, like herself, who do not agree with them. She was also encouraged to understand their view through the lens of their own hurt and perceived neglect by others too.

Exercise 6.2 Embracing Humility

Do you need to be humbler? Do you come across to people as narcissistic or arrogant? Do you tend to have all the answers and none of the questions? Could you ask someone close to you, such as a spouse, best friend, or colleague, how you come across? Could you request, and get, honest feedback from someone? Give it a try. What did they say? Are you surprised by their response to your question? What did you learn from their answers?

_____

_____

_____

_____

_____

The Expectation of Goodness

Often, we expect the worst in others, especially from those who we do not like or understand. We often develop a narrative about people, and if it is a negative one, then we interpret their behaviors through a lens of negativity. We size people up quickly and then try to understand and assimilate information about them through these predetermined narratives, positive or negative (Turiel, 2010).

The third step in this three-step process is to expect the best in people, rather than the worst, and to try to invite that goodness out of them. It suggests that we work to expect and see the goodness from others, even if we disagree with them. It is important to keep in mind that many people, for example, might do the wrong thing for the right reason (Plante & Plante, 2017). For example, college students might drink too much alcohol at a fraternity or sorority party (i.e., a problem behavior that can be very dangerous and even deadly), but they might be doing it in an attempt to be connected to others and develop much needed bonds and intimacy (i.e., a potentially good motive). Students may also do poorly in their classes without the usual parental supervision, sleeping in and missing class, studying for exams, or writing term papers at the last minute (i.e., problem behaviors) but do so in their efforts to become more independent from parents and develop their own schedules and lifestyles (i.e., a potentially good motive).

Thus, people may engage in behaviors that we find problematic, and even offensive, but their motives may not be as bad as they appear on the surface. They may act out of fear, insecurity, immaturity, or lack of adequate information. For example, people may act in ways that are discriminatory towards others, such as people of color. While discrimination is offensive, it may be motivated from the fear of people moving into their community and taking their tenuous jobs away. While the real issue might be fear of losing their job, their concerns are then manifested in discriminatory thinking and behavior from others towards those who are considered a threat. Of course, this tendency does not excuse their behavior or minimize the damage that they might do. It may help to better understand their fears in a way that speaks to their desire for goodness and for a good outcome even if their behavior is on the wrong track and problematic. For example, learning that they resent the competition of immigrants but can see them as human, well-meaning people like themselves is a greatly constructive approach.

Case Example 6.1 James

While it was hard for others to find goodness in James, therapy explored ways to bring goodness out of him. In time, he was ready to have a pet that he could care for and did so with much compassion. He learned to care for a disabled rescue dog that offered him an opportunity to take care of a pet that was rejected and abused by others. He could identify with the dog and learned to care for his pet with compassion. This compassion was then leveraged to encourage and support better behavior towards others.

Case Example 6.2 Quintina

Quintina worked to seek out the goodness in her brothers and highlight the fact that they are all hardworking, kind to their coworkers and families, and would quickly and proudly help a stranger in distress. She decides to attend the holiday celebrations but asks her brothers to limit their conversations to matters other than politics.

Exercise 6.3 Finding Goodness in Others

Review your list of people who you do not like from Exercise 6.1. Although these people represent the group of individuals who you liked the least in your life, make a list of at least three things that are good about them. This may be a challenge to do, but try your best to list at least three qualities that are good about each person.

Six people who you dislike the most	Three qualities you *like* about them
1.	
2.	
3.	
4.	
5.	
6.	

Reflect on this list. Does it alter the way you think about them at all? Why or why not?

_____

_____

_____

_____

_____

Conclusion

Given the extreme divisiveness of our times and the numerous ways that people can think the worst of others, it is critically important for us all to find ways to have productive and respectful conversations with those with whom we disagree. The three-step model of accommodation, humility, and the expectation for goodness can be a helpful framework for thinking through strategies for better conversations and relationships offering helpful and productive tools for conflict resolution, reconciliation, and engagement with difficult others. Trying to understand the views of others, approaching them with humility, and expecting the best from them can potentially turn an explosive and even violent interaction into a salvageable and productive one.

Exercise 6.4 Putting It All Together

Let us put the accommodation, humility, and expectation of goodness to work. Select a person on your list from Exercise 6.1 and try to use this three-step model of accommodation, humility, and the expectation of goodness to move your relationship forward. Could you try to use each of these three steps during your next conversation or engagement with that person? Plan to do so. Once completed, write down what it felt like and what the outcome was for you. Was it helpful? Why or why not?

_____

_____

_____

_____

Further Reading

Exercices Spirituels de Discernement Apostolique en Commun (ESDAC). (2016). Welcoming and building communion together: Manual for facilitators. Author.

Ignatius, St. (2000). *The Spiritual Exercises of St. Ignatius*. Vintage Books.

O'Malley, J. W. (1993). *The first Jesuits*. Harvard University Press.

Further Viewing

Ravizza, Mark, S.J. *Conversations in the Jesuit Tradition*. https://www.youtube.com/watch?v=jAR7q4vE98k.

References

Arthur, C. (2021). *Social warming: The dangerous and polarising effects of social media*. Simon and Schuster.

Bell, W. K. (2018). *The awkward thoughts of W. Kamau Bell: Tales of a 6'4", African American, heterosexual, cisgender, left-leaning, asthmatic, black and proud blerd, mama's boy, dad, and stand-up comedian*. Penguin.

Bilewicz, M., & Soral, W. (2020). Hate speech epidemic: The dynamic effects of derogatory language on intergroup relations and political radicalization. *Political Psychology, 41*(S1), 3–33.

Campbell, W. Keith, Miller, J. D., & Buffardi, L. E. (2010). The United States and the "culture of narcissism": An examination of perceptions of national character. *Social Psychological and Personality Science, 1*(3), 222–229.

Chancellor, J., & Lyubomirsky, S. (2013). Humble beginnings: Current trends, state perspectives, and hallmarks of humility. *Social and Personality Psychology Compass, 7*(11), 819–833.

Fischer, A., Halperin, E., Canetti, D., & Jasini, A. (2018). Why we hate. *Emotion Review, 10*(4), 309–320.

Fiske, S. T. (2000). Stereotyping, prejudice, and discrimination at the seam between the centuries: Evolution, culture, mind, and brain. *European Journal of Social Psychology, 30*(3), 299–322.

Frame, T. (2007). Humility: The despised virtue? *Quadrant, 51*(4), 36–42.

Furedi, F. (2010). Celebrity culture. *Society, 47*(6), 493–497.

Holmes, S., & Redmond, S. (2012). *Framing celebrity: New directions in celebrity culture*. Routledge.

Ignatius, St. (2000). *The Spiritual Exercises of St. Ignatius*. Vintage Books.

Klein, J. L. (2015). Vilifying the pedophiles and perverts: A nationwide test of the Community Attitudes toward Sex Offenders (CATSO) Scale. *Criminology, Criminal Justice Law, & Society, 16*(3), 41–60.

Murray, J. B. (2000). Psychological profile of pedophiles and child molesters. *Journal of Psychology: Interdisciplinary and Applied, 134*(2), 211–224.

O'Malley, J. W. (1993). *The first Jesuits*. Harvard University Press.

Piazza, J. A. (2020). Politician hate speech and domestic terrorism. *International Interactions, 46*(3), 431–453.

Plante, T. G., & Plante, L. G. (2017). *Graduating with honor: Best practices to promote ethics development in college students*. Praeger/ABC-CLIO.

Salter, A. (2018). *Predators: Pedophiles, rapists, and other sex offenders*. Basic Books.

Schaller, M., Park, J., & Faulkner, J. (2003). Prehistoric dangers and contemporary prejudices. *European Review of Social Psychology, 14*(1), 105–137.

Sheth, A., Shalin, V. L., & Kursuncu, U. (2022). Defining and detecting toxicity on social media: context and knowledge are key. *Neurocomputing, 490*, 312–318.

Stalnaker, A. (2008). Judging others: History, ethics, and the purposes of comparison. *Journal of Religious Ethics, 36*(3), 425–444.

Turiel, E. (2010). Snap judgment? Not so fast: Thought, reasoning, and choice as psychological realities. *Human Development, 53*(3), 105–109.

Tyler, I. (2007). From "The Me Decade" to "The Me Millennium": The cultural history of narcissism. *International Journal of Cultural Studies, 10*(3), 343–363.

Van Tongeren, D. R., Davis, D. E., Hook, J. N., & Witvliet, C. V. (2019). Humility. *Current Directions in Psychological Science, 28*(5), 463–468.

Weidman, A. C., Cheng, J. T., & Tracy, J. L. (2018). The psychological structure of humility. *Journal of Personality and Social Psychology, 114*(1), 153–178.

CHAPTER 7

The Pathway to Kinship
Civility, Hospitality, Compassion, Solidarity, and Mutuality

Kinship means experiencing others as brothers and sisters. It suggests that we are all connected and are ultimately extended family. Many diverse spiritual and religious traditions underscore this notion and even agnostic research scientists in fields like genetics, anthropology, and biology often provide compelling evidence that our relationships with each other are biologically closer than many of us assume or believe. Genetic testing using popular saliva-based DNA kits from companies such as Ancestry.com or 23andMe provide affordable and evidence-based data that demonstrates how related most of us are and how many relatives we really have across the world (Hayden, 2017; Hendrickson, 2018; Wynn & Chung, 2017). These companies send customers regular updates typically with intriguing and catchy subject lines such as, "You have more relatives!" Clicking on their updated links reveals that we apparently have many more cousins than we could possibly imagine, and they are typically scattered across the globe. Many of us have also likely played the popular party game often referred to as "six degrees of separation from Kevin Bacon" (Borassi et al., 2014). It demonstrates how through just a few questions regarding mutual connections and experiences, we all have family, friends, and associates in common, and we are surprisingly all more closely connected than imagined (Hautz et al., 2016).

Growing up and attending college in the smallest state in the United States, Rhode Island, and with family who have lived in that state since the 1800s, I often enjoy meeting others from Rhode Island and play the "six degrees of separation" game to see who we know in common. I am rarely disappointed and often am pleasantly surprised that a brief conversation with someone I have never met before who has lived in Rhode Island, or might have some connections there, will often result in having several contacts and even relatives in common. These experiences underscore how connected we all are when we stop to think about it, and we take some time to explore our commonalities with others.

Jesuit spirituality and principles highlight this notion of kinship and attempt to use this perspective to encourage all of us to treat each other better and as family members—brothers and sisters all. Well-known Jesuit priest Fr. Greg Boyle, S.J., frequently speaks and writes about this notion of kinship regarding his remarkable work with former gang members in Los Angeles (Boyle, 2011, 2017). His internationally recognized efforts to help former gang members improve their lives and get jobs associated with his nonprofit company, Homeboy Industries, is an inspiration for many (Choi & Kiesner, 2007). His emphasis on kinship highlights that even gang members who have committed terrible crimes can be rehabilitated, respected, and ultimately transformed (Boyle, 2011, 2017; Pelly & Zhang, 2018). Connection, community-building love, kinship, and a healthy and stable job go a long way in doing so.

Building upon other principles already discussed in previous chapters (e.g., seeing the sacred or divine in all, *curia personalis*, approaching others with accommodation, humility, and the expectation of a kinship perspective) can be very helpful in our relationships with others. It is harder to hate, demonize, harshly judge, and cancel others if you believe that they are your kin—brothers and sisters. A kinship perspective helps to soften our relationships and the conflicts that often emerge within them. It typically means treating everyone with at least civility, respect, and care in mind and as guiding principles of interaction. Highlighting a kinship perspective along with the other principles discussed in this book hopefully will have synergistic effects as well.

The path to a kinship perspective comes in stages, as it is difficult for people to suddenly embrace a kinship way of being and relating to others. These stages include civility, hospitality, compassion, solidarity, and mutuality (Plante, 2019). Embracing each step of these stages leads one to better embrace and maintain a kinship point of view and way of interacting with others. Thus, there is a build-up to kinship that helps all of us maintain and embrace this perspective towards others. Let us now look at what is meant by each of these stages and provide examples as well.

Civility

Sadly, civility is often hard to come by in our rapidly changing and challenging world. Anger and outrage seem to be the order of the day when it comes to divisive politics, social media engagement, and in relations with those we do not like or agree. Certainly, much has been written and discussed about the lack of civility in the workplace, and in society more generally (e.g., Porath, 2015; Porath & Pearson, 2013). Acting in ways that are demeaning, insulting, sarcastic, and aggressive are much more commonplace and have become normalized in much of society. Social media, cable news, talk radio, and well-known celebrities in politics, athletics, entertainment, and business who engage in and are often reinforced for incivility encourage further deterioration of a respectful and polite society (Bowman, 2020). The famous incidents of technology company giants in this regard are often excused as the price of genius and therefore become a model for others to emulate (Brennan-Jobs, 2018; Kantrowitz, 2020). Yet, workplace incivility has been found to take a great toll on employee stress, productivity, turnover, and creativity, having a significant negative impact on employee mental and physical health and well-being (Pearson & Porath, 2009). Tragically, workplace incivility is even associated with fatal errors in hospital environments as well as other serious consequences in many industries (Felblinger, 2009; Pearson & Porath, 2005).

Many organizations, including the American Psychological Association (APA, 2017), have dealt with significant incidents of incivility among their members. One would think that psychologists, of all people, would not have any problems respectfully getting along with each other within their national professional organization. However, they have had many problems in this area that appeared to peak after revelations emerged that several psychologists were involved with state-sponsored torture of detainees in Guantanamo Bay, Cuba, following the terrorist attacks on September 11, 2001 (Gómez et al., 2016; LoCicero et al., 2016). Recently, I was asked to chair an APA working group to address this problem, which resulted in APA-wide approved guidelines for acceptable civil professional behavior (Plante, 2017). Now, every APA board and committee is expected to have a "civility ambassador" who helps to promote the approved civility principles and expectations and offer corrective feedback to members when these norms and guidelines are violated.

The APA Civility Working Group studied and offered operational definitions of both civility and incivility. These include civility guidelines such as (1) disagree with others respectfully, (2) be open to others without hostility, (3) respect diverse views and groups, and (4) offer productive and corrective feedback to those who behave in demeaning, insulting, disrespectful, and discriminatory ways. Operational definitions of incivility include (1) interrupting and talking over others, (2) over-generalizing and offering dispositional character criticisms and attributions, (3) using language that is perceived as being aggressive, sarcastic, or demeaning, and (4) engaging in disrespectful nonverbal behaviors (e.g., eye rolling, loud sighs) (Plante, 2017, 2019). These guidelines have now been made available to all committees, boards, divisions, leadership, and on all association related listservs.

Civility is a low bar for human relationships and yet it is important to find ways to at least proceed from a basis of civility if we hope to achieve a kinship orientation to our relationships. It is a first step, but certainly not the last, in our efforts to promote kinship among each other. Here are a few examples of how civility can be used to help those often not treated in a civil way due to their actions and surroundings.

Case Example 7.2 Juan

Juan is a gang member in Los Angeles who has been in and out of jail during his years on the streets. He has numerous gang-related tattoos, and his family and life circumstances led him to believe that the only way he could survive in the world was to join a gang. He realized that people were uncomfortable and even frightened by him, especially given his appearance, and he was used to people recoiling from him. Juan was involved with a program to get gang members off the streets, out of gangs, and gainfully employed. He knew that if he continued his gang-related activities, he would surely die an early and violent death like so many of his friends and fellow gang members. Juan was assigned to a social worker at the treatment clinic when he was mandated to receive court-ordered psychotherapy as part of his probation plan. He felt pleasantly surprised that the social worker treated him with respect and dignity. Over time, Juan gained trust with the social worker and learned to treat others with civility and respect as well. He learned that there was safety in relationships and not just in instilling fear and distance in others.

Certainly, everyone can be treated in a civil manner, even those who are often treated poorly by society. Civility is a start on the path towards kinship but a necessary one to move to the next stage, hospitality.

Exercise 7.1 Civility in Your Life

Is your life a civil one? Are your interactions with family, friends, coworkers, and customers civil? Are there experiences that you have had that have been uncivil? Name an example of an uncivil encounter?

_____

_____

How did it make you feel?

_____

_____

Were you the victim or perpetrator in the uncivil encounter?

_____

_____

_____

Write down your reflections here.

_____

_____

_____

_____

Exercise 7.2 Civility at Work

Review the civility guidelines from the American Psychological Association discussed above. Would you add or subtract any of them for your use?

_____

_____

Might your work or home environment benefit from using them? Why or why not?

_____

_____

Could you install them as policy in your work or home environment?

_____

_____

_____

Hospitality

Step two on our path to kinship includes hospitality. Jesuit spirituality, as well as many other religious and spiritual traditions, encourage and support a spirit or the charism of hospitality among people and communities, including strangers. A charism of hospitality means that we should be gracious, kind, and welcoming of others, even strangers. In the Jewish tradition, a well-known and often quoted biblical story from Genesis (18:1–15) includes Abraham and his wife, Sarah, welcoming several strangers into their desert tent where they offered them hospitality with rest, food, and drink. Abraham and Sarah did not realize that these strangers were actually angels sent by God (Hartog, 2020) and were honored and rewarded accordingly. In the monastic Christian tradition, the Rules of St. Benedict include treating everyone, again even strangers, as if they are Jesus himself (Frey, 2018; Henry, 2021). This approach was well personified by Saint Brother Alphonsus Rodríguez (1532–1617), who was a well-known Jesuit brother who served as a porter, or a door attendant, at a Jesuit college in Majorca, Spain. He was well known for treating everyone he encountered as if he or she were Jesus, and whenever he heard a knock at the door, he would famously say, "I'm coming, Lord!" These stories, perspectives, and rules provide a template for treating others with hospitality that includes graciousness, generosity, and a welcoming spirit.

We likely all have had moments when we were welcomed and graciously treated by someone when we needed help. We likely fondly remember a time when someone, even a stranger, was unexpectedly kind to us and helped us in some important way at an important time when it was sorely needed. These moments and memories can be powerful ones that are often both remembered and well appreciated for the rest of our lives. Often these moments of hospitality offered by others are just the thing that is needed and offered at just the right time too. They influence us in important and powerful ways. Frequently, they were spontaneous offers of graciousness and may or may not have even been a heavy lift for the person offering us their hospitality.

A hospitable and welcoming spirit connects people and allows them to feel accepted, included, and not judged. It reduces their defenses and opens people up for communication that is more intimate, honest, and caring. Our path towards kinship therefore must include hospitality.

Using our previous example of Juan, let us see how hospitality can be at work in his case.

Case Example 7.1 Juan

Juan was struck by the apology he received when his social worker therapist was 10 minutes late for their scheduled session. He felt that the apology was an important statement: that he, and his time, mattered and that he found it a gracious and hospitable action. He was used to people blowing him off and not showing up when they promised to do so. The apology felt genuine to Juan and was interpreted as a sign of respect and hospitality in his view.

Being offered hospitality is a good feeling, especially for those who are often treated poorly and with a lack of care and concern. It is a necessary part of moving towards kinship, but there are still more steps to go, including compassion, our next step.

Exercise 7.3 Hospitality in Your Life

Think of a time when you were treated with hospitality when you really needed it. Who provided the hospitality to you and why?

_____

_____

How did it feel to receive it?

_____

_____

Exercise 7.4 When Were You Hospitable to Others?

Think of a time when you provided much-needed hospitality to someone else. How did it make you feel?

_____

_____

How did it make them feel?

_____

_____

What were the circumstances for your hospitality?

_____

_____

Compassion

Once civility and hospitality are embraced and practiced, then the third stage on the path to kinship, focusing on compassion, is needed. Compassion is more than just feeling empathy or sympathy for others but is best defined as "being moved by another's suffering and wanting to help" (Lazarus, 1991, p. 298).

Most people would agree that the world needs more compassion, as there are so many people who struggle and suffer mightily. Sadly, we often habituate to the daily news and become immune to the tragic and difficult challenges that many people regularly face. If you hear about or witness suffering on a regular basis, you come to expect it and may not be moved by it. Much has been written on our need to nurture a more compassionate world and how spirituality and the various religious traditions can help us with this important goal. In fact, popular religion writer and scholar Karen Armstrong's classic book, _The Great Transformation: The Beginning of Our Religious Traditions_ (Armstrong, 2006), states that the most important and fundamental unifying trait of all of the world's major religious traditions is actually compassion. Of course, all the religious traditions have had their terrible moments over the centuries where egregious acts were committed without any compassion at all. At times, religious communities and leaders have nurtured hate and cruelty. This continues even today in many parts of the world. However, at their best and most fundamental, the religious and spiritual traditions have highlighted, focused on, and aspired toward compassion (Armstrong 2006).

Jesuit spirituality, the focus of this book, has frequently highlighted compassion as well. In fact, the goal at Santa Clara University, a Catholic and Jesuit university where I have worked for 30 years, is to educate leaders to be people of "competence, conscience, and compassion"—the 3 Cs. The global network of Jesuit education and spirituality highlights the importance of compassion and often invokes biblical passages to support this important and critical perspective, such as the writing of St. Paul, including: "Clothe yourselves with compassion, kindness, humility, gentleness, and patience" (Colossians 3:12) as well as "Be kind to one another, compassionate, and mutually forgiving ..." (Ephesians 4:32).

Many people nowadays emphasize and underscore the importance of self-compassion (Neff, 2011; Neff & Knox, 2020). Research has found that self-compassion can be helpful to many in taking better care of themselves, improving their self-esteem, and enhancing their self-forgiveness (Germer & Neff, 2019). Self-compassion, while certainly important and needed by many, should be balanced with compassion for others in order to avoid potential narcissism and self-centeredness that can occur if the compassion focus is only about ourselves alone (Demirci et al., 2019).

Again, using our previous example of Juan, let us see how compassion can be put to good use in his case.

Case Example 7.1 Juan

Juan decided that he could help others leave gang activities. He wanted to become a mentor to the new recruits in the program to help move local gang members into more productive ways of living, being, and working. He claimed that he felt like a big brother to some of these younger gang members and believed that his efforts and the compassion that he offered were helpful to them. He boasted that these efforts might even save some lives in the process.

Exercise 7.5 Compassion in Your Life

Think of a time when you were treated with compassion when you really needed it. Who provided the compassion to you, and why?

_____

_____

_____

How did it feel to receive it?

_____

_____

_____

Exercise 7.6 When Were You Compassionate to Others?

Think of a time when you provided much-needed compassion to someone else. How did it make you feel?

_____

_____

How did it make them feel?

_____

_____

What were the circumstances for your compassion?

_____

_____

_____

Compassion is needed before moving on to our next step towards kinship, which focuses on solidarity and mutuality.

Solidarity and Mutuality

Solidarity and mutuality are other important concepts that must occur and be fully embraced on our path towards kinship. Solidarity and mutuality recognize that we all are equals and that our lives are interconnected in important ways that might not seem readily obvious to us upon first glance (Ederer, 1991; Kolvenbach, 2008). Solidarity and mutuality with others mean that we stand *with* and *by* others, especially with those who are struggling or marginal.

People often feel bad for others who are struggling and might have a desire to help them in some way. Perhaps they want to offer money or their time to be of help. While compassion, empathy, and a desire to help others might be a noble and welcomed quality in people, if their efforts are conducted in a way that highlights their superiority or good fortune, then their efforts can be perceived as insulting and thus not offered in the spirit of solidarity, mutuality, and kinship. Sometimes people who have many resources and are interested in helping those who are struggling can act as if they are a bull in a china shop. They may swoop in and quickly assess what the problems are and what the solutions should be. This can be very insulting and off-putting to those they are trying to help. They may come across as being arrogant, narcissistic, and smug. While people might appreciate their efforts or their motivations, they approach others with an air of superiority, acting as if they know better than anyone else about how to potentially solve problems they do not fully understand or appreciate. Fr. Greg Boyle underscores that if you approach others who are on the margins with humility, openness, mutuality, and solidarity, then everyone is better served.

Solidarity and mutuality mean that we are deeply respectful to those we wish to serve, and we must try and fully understand them and their predicament in a way that embraces our humility and lack of genuine appreciation for their struggles. Mutuality means that we can all learn from each other and grow from our interactions and communications. We learn from and help each other regardless of our power, status, and resources.

Once again, our example of Juan can prove instructive in how solidarity and mutuality can be used for transformation.

Case Example 7.1 Juan

Juan stated that the notion of solidarity struck a familiar chord in him as a former gang member in that gang members learn to stick together and stand up for each other. That said, he also understood that solidarity in gangs resulted in crime and murders, too. He learned that solidarity and mutuality can be experienced in a more positive and healthy way. The notion of solidarity learned through gang involvement could be altered in a more positive way and could help him connect and relate to the younger gang members that he was now trying to help. He stated that he understood their world and their challenges and that he could offer his support and solidarity as they tried to find a more productive and safe way of being.

Exercise 7.7 Solidarity and Mutuality in Your Life

Have you even engaged in volunteerism? If so, who were you working with?

_____

Reflect on the interactions you had in your volunteer efforts. Were they mutually beneficial? Were they based in solidarity?

_____

_____

Were these activities more about you and your needs or were they about the needs of others?

_____

How did you feel about your efforts?

_____

_____

Now that we have addressed these steps of civility, hospitality, compassion, solidarity, and mutuality, we are now ready to nurture kinship.

Finally, Kinship

Once civility, hospitality, solidarity, and mutuality are embraced and practiced, we can then achieve kinship, treating others as brothers and sisters. This approach and perspective have enormous implications in how we interact with others. They certainly can create a better and more connected community, alter the way people interact with one another, and even potentially transform society if supported on a grand scale. Social media would be a kinder and gentler place as would our work and home environments if a kinship perspective was prioritized (Boyle, 2011, 2017).

Exercise 7.8 Kindship with Others

Using a 10-point scale with 10 being very high and 1 being very low, what degree of kinship do you feel with your family? _____ Coworkers? _____ Neighbors? _____ Strangers? _____

If you offered low numbers (e.g., 1–5) for any of these groups of people, what prevents you from feeling more kinship for them?

_____

_____

Could you do more to increase your numbers for each of these categories? Why or why not?

_____

_____

_____

_____

Conclusion

Human relationships can be enhanced if we maintain a path towards kinship. If we can treat others as family—brothers and sisters—we can improve many of the challenges that we often face in our relationships. However, this perspective is not easy to maintain given how difficult it can be to maintain healthy and productive relationships with people in our lives whom we may not like or agree with on important matters. A pathway that includes civility, hospitality, compassion, solidarity, and mutuality is necessary and important to highlight, embrace, and nurture. If we are successful in these endeavors, a rewarding community that fosters and nurtures kinships becomes possible.

Further Reading

Boyle, G. (2011). *Tattoos on the heart: The power of boundless compassion.* Simon and Schuster.

Boyle, G. (2017). *Barking to the choir: The power of radical kinship.* Simon and Schuster.

Plante, T. G. (Ed.). (2015). *The psychology of compassion and cruelty: Understanding the emotional, spiritual, and religious influences.* Praeger/ABC-CLIO.

References

American Psychological Association. (2017). Ethical principles of psychologists and code of conduct (2002, amended effective June 1, 2010, and January 1, 2017). https://www.apa.org/about/policy/palliative-care-eol

Armstrong, K. (2006). The great transformation: The beginning of our religious traditions. Anchor Books.

Borassi, M., Crescenzi, P., Habib, M., Kosters, W. A., Marino, A., & Takes, F. (2014, July). On the solvability of the six degrees of Kevin Bacon game. International Conference on Fun with Algorithms (pp. 52–63).

Bowman, R. (2020). Civility can be taught and learned. *Education, 140*(2), 80–86.

Brennan-Jobs, L. (2018). *Small fry: A memoir.* Grove Press.

Choi, D. Y., & Kiesner, F. (2007). Homeboy Industries: An incubator of hope and businesses. *Entrepreneurship Theory and Practice, 31*(5), 769–786.

Demirci, I., Eksi, H., & Eksi, F. (2019). Narcissism, life satisfaction, and harmony: The mediating role of self-esteem and self-compassion. *Eurasian Journal of Educational Research, 19*(84), 159–176.

Ederer, R. J. (1991). Heinrich Pesch, solidarity, and social encyclicals. *Review of Social Economy, 49*(4), 596–610.

Felblinger, D. M. (2009). Bullying, incivility, and disruptive behaviors in the healthcare setting: Identification, impact, and intervention. *Frontiers of Health Services Management, 25*(4), 13–23.

Frey, S. M. (2018). Humility rules: Saint Benedict's twelve-step guide to genuine self-esteem. *Catholic Library World, 88*(3), 215.

Germer, C., & Neff, K. (2019). Teaching the mindful self-compassion program: A guide for professionals. Guilford Press.

Gómez, J. M., Smith, C. P., Gobin, R. L., Tang, S. S., & Freyd, J. J. (2016). Collusion, torture, and inequality: Understanding the actions of the American Psychological Association as institutional betrayal. *Journal of Trauma & Dissociation, 17*(5), 527–544.

Hartog, P. (2020). Abraham and the Rhetoric of Hospitality and Foreignness in Hebrews and 1 Clement. *Science et Esprit, 72*(3), 281–296.

Hautz, W. E., Krummrey, G., Exadaktylos, A., & Hautz, S. C. (2016). Six degrees of separation: the small world of medical education. *Medical Education, 50*(12), 1274–1279.

Hayden, E. C. (2017). The rise and fall and rise again of 23andMe. *Nature, 550*(7675), 174–177.

Hendrickson, N. (2018). *Unofficial guide to Ancestry.com: How to find your family history on the #1 genealogy website* (2nd ed.). Penguin.

Henry, P. (2021). *Benedictine options: Learning to live from the sons and daughters of Saints Benedict and Scholastica.* Liturgical Press.

Kantrowitz, A. (2020). *Always day one: How the tech titans plan to stay on top forever.* Penguin.

Kolvenbach, P.-H. (2008). The service of faith and promotion of justice in American higher education. In G. W. Traub, *A Jesuit education reader* (pp. 144–162). Loyola Press.

Lazarus, R. (1991). *Emotion and adaptation.* Oxford University Press.

LoCicero, A., Marlin, R. P., Jull-Patterson, D., Sweeney, N. M., Gray, B. L., & Boyd, J. W. (2016). Enabling torture: APA, clinical psychology training and the failure to disobey. *Peace and Conflict: Journal of Peace Psychology, 22*(4), 345–355.

Neff, K. D. (2011). Self-compassion, self-esteem, and well-being. *Social and Personality Psychology Compass, 5*(1), 1–12.

Neff, K., & Knox, M. C. (2020). Self-compassion. In T. K. Shackelford & V. Zeigler-Hill (Eds.), *Encyclopedia of Personality and Individual Differences* (pp. 4663–4670). Springer.

Pearson, C. M., & Porath, C. L. (2005). On the nature, consequences and remedies of workplace incivility: No time for "nice"? Think again. *Academy of Management Executive, 19*(1), 7–18.

Pearson, C., & Porath, C. (2009). *The cost of bad behavior: How incivility is damaging your business and what to do about it.* Penguin.

*Pelly, R. D. M., & Zhang, Y. (2018). Homeboy Industries: Redefining social responsibility. *Journal of Case Research and Inquiry, 4*(17), 17–48.

Plante, T. G. (2017). Making APA civil again: The efforts and outcomes of the civility working group. *Professional Psychology: Research and Practice, 48*(6), 401–404.

Plante, T. G. (2019). Possible next steps in APA's civility efforts: Moving from civility to hospitality, solidarity, and to kinship. *The Specialist, 44,* 23–26.

Porath, C. (2015, March 11). The leadership behavior that's most important to employees. *Harvard Business Review.* Retrieved October 11, 2016, from https://hbr.org/2015/05/the-leadership-behavior-thats-most-important-to-employees.

Porath, C., & Pearson, C. (2013). The price of incivility. *Harvard Business Review, 91*(1–2), 114–121.

*Santa Clara University. www.scu.edu.

Wynn, J., & Chung, W. K. (2017). 23andMe paves the way for direct-to-consumer genetic health risk tests of limited clinical utility. *Annals of Internal Medicine, 167*(2), 125–126.

CHAPTER 8

Ethics

All the spiritual and religious traditions offer strategies and guidelines for how we should live our lives and behave in the world (Sia, 2008). They provide guidance for decision making and tend to highlight various virtues, such as honesty, integrity, generosity, compassion, and humility. The spiritual and religious traditions are full of stories, parables, and commandments that outline a plan and path to live an ethical and righteous life. Jesuit spirituality is not unique in its emphasis on ethics. It is one part of the choir of voices singing the same song about how to live in the world and how to use principles discussed in sacred scripture and elsewhere for living an ethical life.

Ethics is defined as principles, strategies, and rules for living (Rachels & Rachels, 2012; Vaughn, 2015). Alternatively, as Socrates famously asked, "How ought we to live?" (Vlastos, 1991). One does not necessarily need to be affiliated with or embrace a particular spiritual or religious tradition to support ethical living (Nielsen, 2010). However, these age-old wisdom and faith traditions offer much to say about ethics and have been fine-tuning their efforts for hundreds, if not thousands, of years (Lama, 2012). The academic and applied fields of ethics (e.g., biological, business, legal) are offshoots of moral philosophy and are usually focused on either theoretical or applied ethical decision making about various conflicts and challenges that we experience (Hutcheson, 2006).

In this chapter, we look at strategies for ethical living that can be applied to useful decision making. Mostly, we will focus on virtues that act as guideposts and motivators. We will see that most of the general decision making that we make can be viewed through an ethical lens. Thus, being introduced to and well versed in strategies for ethical decision making can be helpful in all our decisions.

Many centuries of reflection and writing in moral philosophy and ethics have resulted in several key principles for ethical decision making and ethical consideration (Rachels & Rachels, 2012; Vaughn, 2015). Most of these principles fall into two major categories: consequential and nonconsequential ethics. Consequential ethics highlight good outcomes or preferred results while nonconsequential ethics underscore good principles without particular concern for the actual outcomes they might achieve. For example, a utilitarian perspective would seek to find solutions that would result in a good outcome pleasing to most people (e.g., voting on an issue so that the majority of people get their way). An absolute moral or Kantian perspective would follow a given rule or dictate regardless of the resulting outcome (e.g., always tell the truth no matter what the outcome might be).

Before examining particular ethical strategies that can be used in decision making, let us review the major general approaches to ethics.

General Approaches to Ethical Decision Making
Egoism

It may be surprising to many that egoism is the most common approach to ethical decision making used by people to make hard decisions (Feinberg, 2007; Vaughn, 2015). Egoism is considering and acting upon what is in your best interest. People may act ethically or appropriately in ways that simply serve their best interests. They may be honest to avoid having to deal with a guilty conscience or the burden of keeping track of their lies. They may donate to charity to take a tax write-off. They may express care and concern to others to signal their virtue as being a nice and caring person. Egoism is a reasonable approach to ethical decision making since the outcomes, regardless of the motivations for behaving in a particular way, can be good outcomes for all (Rachels & Rachels, 2012). Thus, egoism is a consequential approach to ethics in that it is a strategy where the outcome matters most. If someone wants to donate a large amount of money to a worthy cause to get a tax write-off and perhaps see their name in the news or etched on a major building, they may be making the world a better place. They are helping others but helping themselves too.

Whether or not people act on their egoism impulses, they certainly consider them as they make challenging decisions. For example, in my over 30 years of teaching ethics at Stanford and Santa Clara Universities, I have never had a student reflect on ethical decision-making options without at least considering using egoism to maximize their own self-interest (Plante, 2004). What is in it for me is the theme of egoism, but what is in your best interest can also be in the best interest of others too.

Exercise 8.1 Egoism in Your Life

Think of a generous or gracious act you did recently. Perhaps it was donating to a worthy cause or offering to help a friend, coworker, or family member in need. Was your behavior motivated by egoism at all?

_____

What did you get out of the act? Be honest with yourself.

_____

Repeat this exercise with several more altruistic acts that you can remember. Can you see how egoism might impact your behavior? Why or why not?

_____

_____

_____

_____

Subjectivism

Subjectivism is doing what feels right in the moment. In addition to egoism, subjectivism is the most common way of making ethical decisions for people (Rachels & Rachels, 2012; Vaughn, 2015). The approach depends on emotions and thinking in the moment that requires little careful or deep thought or reflection. It follows the notion that if it feels right or seems right, then just do it. Like egoism, subjectivism is a consequential approach to ethics in that it highlights good outcomes in the best interest of the decision maker rather than following a particular moral or ethical principle regardless of where the principle leads one in their decision-making outcomes.

Exercise 8.2 Subjectivism in Your Life

How do you tend to make ethical or moral decisions? Do you do what feels right in the moment?

_____

Think of a moral or ethical dilemma you have had recently. It could be something big or little. How did you decide how you should handle it? Did subjectivism guide your thinking? Why or why not?

_____

_____

_____

_____

_____

Cultural Relativism

Cultural relativism refers to the fact that different cultures, broadly defined, have different ways of doing things while considering challenging ethical matters (Rachels & Rachels, 2012; Vaughn, 2015). These cultural differences may be influenced by ethnicity, race, religion, country or location of origin, gender, socioeconomic status, and numerous other categories that define culture and diversity (Brown, 2008; Healy, 2007). For example, those who come from communal cultures may have very different ways of thinking about ethical challenges than those who come from more individualistic cultures. Cultural differences can be subtle as well, and there may be a great deal of diversity within as well as between different cultural groups and communities. Cultural relativism suggests that ethical challenges and decisions should be made with the cultural context in mind and that approaching others with some degree of cultural respect and humility is important (Davis et al., 2021).

Exercise 8.3 Cultural Relativism and You

How would you describe your cultural background?

_____

Is it based on race, religion, ethnicity, gender, or country or geographical location of origin?

_____

Which group or with what culture most influences you and your identity?

_____

What is unique about your culture and identification as they relate to ethical decision making?

_____

Write down how your primary cultural identity and influence and how they inform your decision making.

_____

_____

What have you learned through this reflection and exercise?

_____

_____

_____

_____

Utilitarianism

Utilitarianism looks to provide the most happiness for the most people (Rachels & Rachels, 2012; Scarre, 2020; Vaughn, 2015). It is democratic in that it seeks to please more people than not, and it is a consequentialist approach to ethics in terms of seeking good outcomes rather than following a particular ethical path. Utilitarianism suggests that the most ethical decision will be the one that makes the most people happy in any situation.

Exercise 8.4 Utilitarianism and You

Think amount a recent ethical or moral decision that you made. Were you concerned about pleasing people while you made the decision?

_____

Do you generally try to please the most people when making decisions?

_____

Why or why not?

_____

_____

_____

Absolute Moral Rules

Absolute moral rules are a nonconsequential approach to ethical decision making. They state that one should follow moral rules regardless of their consequences (Baron, 2018; Rachels & Rachels, 2012; Vaughn, 2015). For example, always telling the truth may be a common absolute moral rule, but it might have negative consequences if truth-telling results in people being hurt or even killed under certain circumstances. The absolute moral rule approach does allow exceptions to rules under certain circumstances, but, overall, it encourages people to follow certain rules regardless of consequences (Baron, 2018; Stern, 2015).

Exercise 8.5 Your Absolute Moral Rules

Do you have any absolute moral rules that guide your decision making?

_____

Do you have rules that are just not negotiable?

_____

If so, what are they?

_____

Why are they important to you?

_____

_____

_____

Justice

The justice approach to ethics highlights what is fair (Rachels & Rachels, 2012; Vaughn, 2015). Injustices can come in many forms, and people may be either greatly harmed or benefit from social and personal injustices. Racism, discrimination, financial, and societal privileges are all ethical issues related to justice. Sometimes there is tension regarding an ethics of justice versus ethics of care in many fields in that what might be fair might not ultimately be caring (Botes, 2000).

Exercise 8.6 Justice in Your Life

Think of a time when you benefited from an injustice. Perhaps a friend or relative did you a favor that benefited you in a way that was not an option for others. How did it make you feel to receive the benefits of an injustice?

_____

How about a time when you were victimized by an injustice? Can you think of a time when you were treated unjustly? How did that make you feel?

_____

_____

_____

Social Contract

Social contracts are those informal ethical rules and guidelines that we come to accept and embrace as a community (Rachels & Rachels, 2012; Vaughn, 2015). These may include "first come, first serve" when you wait in line at a coffee shop or a grocery store or making reservations ahead of time on airplanes and at restaurants to secure a spot for the day and time that you desire. While there may not be any laws or specific rules about these matters, there are informal social norms that guide our behavior (Jos, 2006; Muldoon, 2016).

Exercise 8.7 Social Contract and You

What social contracts operate in your life? What informal or societal rules do you follow routinely?

_____

Why are they important to you?

_____

What would happen if you failed to follow them?

_____

_____

_____

_____

Common Good

The common good approach to ethics involves what is in the best interest of our entire community— locally, regionally, and even globally (Rachels & Rachels, 2012; Vaughn, 2015). The common good approach, for example, would suggest that we should be careful with our carbon footprint, recycling all that we can and avoiding consuming fossil fuels and other polluting products (Hollenbach & Hollenbach, 2002). The common good approach would suggest that we seek out educational and employment opportunities that can help to create a better world for everyone rather than seeking options that only help ourselves.

Exercise 8.8 The Common Good and You

What do you do for the common good?

_____

Why do you do what you do for the common good?

_____

Is there something that you could do more for the common good? If so, what is it?

_____

What prevents you from doing it?

_____

_____

Rights

The rights approach speaks to various rights that we hold near and dear (Rachels & Rachels, 2012; Vaughn, 2015). These might include the right to "life, liberty, and the pursuit of happiness" as our American founding fathers proclaimed (Rezek et al., 2011). Other rights might include freedom of speech, and the rights to vote, receive a living wage, obtain adequate food, and reasonable housing (Bunge, 1989). The rights approach to ethics also includes equal rights for men and women or for the rich and poor.

Exercise 8.9 Rights and You

What rights do you hold near and dear? What rights do you have or wished that you had that really matter to you?

_____

Why are they so important?

_____

_____

Virtue

The virtue approach highlights values that help guide our thinking and behavior (Hursthouse, 1999; Rachels & Rachels, 2012; Vaughn, 2015). There is a long list of possible virtues that we might embrace and use in our ethical decision-making processes (Trianosky, 1990). These include, as examples, honesty, integrity, gratitude, graciousness, responsibility, accountability, competence, compassion, and so forth. In psychology and related fields (e.g., social work, marriage and family therapy, counseling), our organizational code of ethics tends to highlight a virtue approach to ethics that is articulated and expanded upon in our respective ethical writings, rules, and codes (DiFranks, 2008; Kelly, 2001; Young, 2017). A review of them shows that the following five virtues are most often highlighted in all these ethical guidelines: respect, responsibility, integrity, competence, and concern for others (Plante, 2004). These five principles for ethical behavior within our professional codes can be easily remembered using the acronym RRICC (i.e., respect, responsibility, integrity, competence, and concern). Perhaps even easier to remember that further highlights a virtue approach to the mental health professional's code of ethics is respect and compassion.

Most organizations, companies, small and large businesses, schools, universities, and so forth highlight several virtues that they most especially embrace (Alegre et al., 2018; Davis et al., 2007). They are often included in their mission and identity statements, websites, and advertising efforts. These are aspirational principles and values that are hopefully taken seriously and not mere lip service to enhance these organizations' images and profits (King et al., 2010).

For example, in Jesuit circles there are virtues and value statements that are frequently invoked to represent the aspirations near and dear to these institutions). They include, for example, gratitude, generosity of spirit, and men and women for and with others (Kirby et al., 2006). At Santa Clara University, for example, we claim to be people of "competence, conscience, and compassion" and we strive to build a "more humane, just, and sustainable world" (see Santa Clara University; Korth, 2008; Plante & Plante, 2017).

These various approaches to ethics can be tools in the ethical toolbox when reflecting upon and trying to decide how best to proceed with ethical dilemmas and challenges. Various approaches can be considered before decisions are made. In the next section, we will consider a five-step process for ethical decision making.

Exercise 8.10 Your Virtues

What would you say are your top three virtues that are most important to you? Write them down.

Your Top Three Virtues

1. _____

2. _____

3. _____

Why are they so important to you?

_____

_____

Do you live your life with these in mind to guide you? Why or why not?

_____

_____

_____

The Five-Step Process for Ethical Decision Making

There is a well-established five-step model for making ethical decisions that is used by most people in the field of ethics (Knapp et al., 2017). It includes (1) recognizing that an ethical issue exists, (2) getting the facts, (3) considering various ethical approaches to solve the dilemma, (4) making a decision, and (5) considering the decision in retrospect. Let us now review each of these stages to see what they offer us in our ethical decision-making process.

1. Recognizing an Ethical Issue

People are often completely unaware that they are experiencing an ethical challenge or dilemma. The first step in ethical decision making is being more mindful that ethical issues are all around us and that we face ethical issues daily. Ethics are everywhere and present themselves in obvious but typically more subtle ways all the time. Many people might only pay attention to large and significant ethical problems such as marital infidelity, cheating on taxes, and stealing goods and services as common examples. They may not notice more subtle or less obvious ethical challenges. Thus, the first step in ethical decision making is to notice that they are around us all the time.

For example, I have been teaching classes on ethics at Stanford University Medical School as well as Santa Clara University for over three decades (Plante & Pistoresi, 2017). When we start class early in the academic term, I often ask students what ethical dilemmas they may have experienced in the past day or two. At the beginning of the term, they rarely have anything to report. Yet, as the term moves forward, they find themselves being more attentive to ethical issues and typically have many ethical challenges to report by the time the class ends. These students have developed the sensitivity to see the world through an ethical lens and thus notice both subtle and less subtle ethical issues and challenges on a regular basis (Plante, 1995, 1998).

2. Getting the Facts

To avoid simply acting on impulse and emotion, it is important to get the facts before making an ethical decision. Sometimes facts are hard to come by or they are questionable. However, it is important to do our due diligence in finding out all that we can to make an informed, thoughtful, and evidence-based ethical decision. We should be careful to avoid appeals to emotion or the need to take immediate actions to carefully be sure that we have all of the information that we need, and that our information is both reliable and valid, in order to make a good decision.

3. Considering Various Ethical Approaches

As mentioned earlier in this chapter, there are a variety of principles, strategies, or tools to help us make good ethical decisions. When confronted with an ethical dilemma, one can apply both consequential and nonconsequential strategies to think through the problem. We can use utilitarianism, justice, the common good, a social contract, absolute moral rules, cultural relativism, and virtue approaches, to name just a few (Vaughn, 2015). If we use various approaches in our ethical decision making, we may find that some approaches lead us to one set of actions while another ethical approach might lead us to a completely different set of actions. This potential conflict is helpful as we can then think through the pros and cons, costs, and benefits of each approach more carefully.

4. Making a Decision

One can only consider various points of view for so long as decisions typically must be made—and often quickly. Ultimately, we need to act and sometimes do so with less-than-ideal information to go on or with a confident plan for action. I remember a conversation with a friend who was a pediatric kidney transplant surgeon at Stanford who was interested in ethics who said that in his world, decisions in medicine must be made extremely quickly (e.g., Should we conduct this emergency surgery now?). Thus, one cannot reflect and debate for very long as philosophers and ethicists often encourage us to do so. He has an excellent point. We frequently are broad sided with an ethical dilemma that needs a quick response and resolution. Thus, we need to build enough ethical muscle to have the experience and instincts to make good decisions quickly and often in unexpected and challenging circumstances.

5. Considering Our Decisions in Retrospect

The final stage in ethical decision making is the consideration of our decisions in retrospect. As we reflect on our ethical decision-making process and outcomes, we might ask ourselves if we made a good decision in hindsight. Were there unexpected consequences of our decision making? Is there something to learn from our experience so that we might be able to make a better decision next time? We want to be sure that we learn from our experiences in ethical decision making so that we continue to improve upon our skills and build more ethical muscles over time.

Exercise 8.11 Trying Out the Five-Step Model in Your Life

Let's try using this five-step model in your life. Can you think of an ethical dilemma that you have had recently? Go through the five-step model to think through a best way to deal with it.

_____

What have you learned from your process?

_____

_____

_____

Now that we have discussed various approaches to ethical decision making and the process for making ethical decisions, we can examine how spirituality can assist us in using ethics in the psychotherapeutic endeavor.

Spiritual and Religious Ethics Underscore Virtue Ethics

Religious and spiritual traditions tend to be especially supportive of a virtue approach to ethics. These traditions tend to highlight and encourage virtue such as honesty, humility, compassion, forgiveness, and reconciliation. As mentioned earlier, well-known religion writer and scholar Karen Armstrong claims that compassion is at the heart of all the major religious traditions (Armstrong, 2006). Sacred scripture and other spiritual writings within all the religious and spiritual traditions speak to the development of virtue and how these virtues can be further developed, practiced, and embraced by everyone (Davis et al., 2012).

For example, in the Christian New Testament, much is made of "fruits of the spirit." Fruits of the spirit include the virtues and qualities that can be expected with sincere adherence to spiritual and religious teachings and engagement (Caldecott, 2010; Keating, 2000). In St. Paul's letter to the Galatians, he states, "But the fruit of the Spirit is love, joy, peace, patience, kindness, goodness, faithfulness, gentleness, self-control; against such things there is no law" (Galatians 5:22–23).

Jesuit spirituality, among other traditions, highlights and encourages these fruits of the spirit that can be well integrated into our regular and secular lives. Throughout our decision-making process, we often try to answer the question "Who am I and who do I want to be?" You may experience a variety of difficulties and challenges within yourself or in relationships with others that demand careful and thoughtful consideration of next steps and actions about the kind of person you really are or wish to become. Ethical decision making helps us to answer and demonstrate important and fundamental questions about our personal character. Attending to the virtues highlighted in the spiritual and religious wisdom traditions can be helpful in guiding us. While there are many virtues to consider, I will highlight a few of those that are often discussed in Jesuit spirituality that can be applied to ethical decision making.

Gratitude

Much has been studied, written, and discussed about gratitude (Emmons & McCullough, 2004). Often, we can be so focused on what is going wrong in our lives that we fail to see what is going right. Do we tend to see the glass as being half empty or half full? Research has supported efforts to help our clients reflect on what they are grateful for in their lives (Bono et al., 2004; Rash et al., 2011). This is a virtue that can help people cope better with the stresses and strains of life and reorient their perspective towards a more positive outlook (Emmons & Crumpler, 2000). It is also one of the key first steps in the Examen discussed earlier in this book (Manney, 2011).

Exercise 8.12 Gratitude and You

What or who are you grateful for? List five things or people that you are most grateful for.

1. _____

2. _____

3. _____

4. _____

5. _____

What makes you especially grateful for this list?

_____

_____

_____

What might you be able to do to express your gratitude?

_____

_____

_____

Forgiveness

There has been an explosion of research and writing on the benefits of forgiveness (Worthington, 2007, 2013). It is a foil to the anger and bitterness that many people hold onto that ultimately harms them (Akhtar & Barlow, 2018). As the popular saying goes, "Anger and bitterness is like drinking poison hoping that the other person will get sick" (Ghezzi, 1980, p. 99). Letting go of anger, bitterness, and resentment has been proven to be therapeutic for many (Enright, 2019; Worthington, 2007, 2013). Forgiveness is a process and is not an all-or-nothing effort. Many people may not be able to fully forgive others for the harm that they caused, but working towards forgiveness can be helpful to lessen the emotional turmoil that resentment can cause (Enright, 2019; Worthington, 2007, 2013).

Exercise 8.13 Who Do You Need to Forgive?

Who in your life do you need to forgive? Who has wronged you in a way that has left you angry, bitter, and resentful?

_____

What did they do?

_____

_____

How has your anger and upset impacted you?

_____

Is there any possibility for forgiveness and reconciliation? Why or why not?

_____

_____

Compassion

Compassion is an important virtue that often seems harder to come by today. Discussed in the previous chapter, there is a great deal of research on the benefits of developing and nurturing compassion in others. Nurturing and supporting compassion with our relationships with others are important tools for better relationships and for well-being (Gilbert, 2005; Plante, 2015).

Exercise 8.14 Compassion in Your Life

Think about a time when you experienced compassion from someone else. How did it make you feel?

_____

Now think about a time when you expressed compassion to someone else. How do you think it made them feel?

_____

How did you feel?

_____

Is there a way to expand your expression of compassion to more people?

_____

What obstacles get in the way of doing so?

_____

_____

_____

People for and with Others

Highlighting the virtue of being there for others in solidarity and support is another important virtue that you might consider. It is a foil to the overly self-focused, narcissistic, and self-centered ways of being in the world. Attending to others can help us to get out of our narrow worldview and self-absorption. Ultimately, it can be therapeutic for us to experience the value of helping others (Black & Living, 2004; Kirby et al., 2006).

Exercise 8.15 Being There for Others

Have you ever engaged in volunteerism or worked with those who might be marginalized in some way?

_____

What did it feel like to do so?

_____

How were your efforts received?

_____

_____

The Magis

The *magi* means "the more." It refers to striving to be better, more helpful, engaged, virtuous, ethical, helpful, and so forth (McKinney, 2009; Mescher, 2018). It suggests that we do not rest on our laurels but rather seek continual self-improvement in who we are and who we want to be. "Magis is a duty to defend human dignity, deliver on human rights and responsibilities, and dedicate ourselves to the common good of all" (Mescher, 2018, p. 39). This virtue can help us continue to work to be better people and make better decisions in multiple ways.

Exercise 8.16 What Do We Need to Do to Be Better?

What do you need to do to be a better person in your life? What could you do to improve upon who you are and what you are about?

_____

_____

_____

_____

List goals for yourself here.

Goals to be a Better Person

1. _____

2. _____

3. _____

4. _____

5. _____

Are these goals doable for you? If not, why not?

_____

_____

_____

_____

Many additional virtues that the spiritual and religious traditions endorse and promote can be well integrated into our ethical decision making. Although they may be based on spiritual and religious thinking, scripture, and ways of thinking, they all can be presented and used in secular ways to help us make better and more ethical decisions.

Conclusion

Religious and spiritual traditions offer a great deal of wisdom about maximizing moral and ethical behavior. Moral philosophy also helps us to reflect upon a variety of ethical strategies for living. In our increasingly troubled and conflicted world, we perhaps need these principles more than ever. Ethical guidelines offered by these religious and spiritual traditions can easily be secularized to appeal to nonreligious and nonspiritual audiences and communities. Embracing helpful ethical strategies for living and using them in our day-to-day lives would likely be an important and positive contribution for a better life for everyone.

Further Reading

Enright, R. D. (2019). *Forgiveness is a choice: A step-by-step process for resolving anger and restoring hope.* American Psychological Association.

Gilbert, P. (Ed.). (2005). *Compassion: Conceptualisations, research and use in psychotherapy.* Routledge.

Hursthouse, R. (1999). *On virtue ethics.* Oxford University Press.

Hutcheson, F. (2006). *A system of moral philosophy.* A&C Black.

Lama, D. (2012). *Beyond religion: Ethics for a whole world.* Houghton Mifflin.

Nielsen, K. (1990). *Ethics without God* (rev. ed.). Prometheus Books.

Plante, T. G. (2004). *Do the right thing: Living ethically in an unethical world.* New Harbinger.

Plante, T. G. (Ed.). (2015). *The psychology of compassion and cruelty: Understanding the emotional, spiritual, and religious influences.* Praeger/ABC-CLIO.

Plante, T. G., & Plante, L. G. (2017). *Graduating with honor: Best practices to promote ethics development in college students.* Praeger/ABC-CLIO.

Rachels, J., & Rachels, S. (2012). *The elements of moral philosophy* (7th ed.). McGraw-Hill.

Vaughn, L. (2015). *Beginning ethics: An introduction to moral philosophy.* Norton.

Worthington, J. (2013). *Forgiveness and reconciliation: Theory and application.* Routledge.

References

Akhtar, S., & Barlow, J. (2018). Forgiveness therapy for the promotion of mental well-being: A systematic review and meta-analysis. *Trauma, Violence, & Abuse, 19*(1), 107–122.

Alegre, I., Berbegal-Mirabent, J., Guerrero, A., & Mas-Machuca, M. (2018). The real mission of the mission statement: A systematic review of the literature. *Journal of Management & Organization, 24*(4), 456–473.

Armstrong, K. (2006). *The great transformation: The beginning of our religious traditions.* Anchor Books.

Baron, M. W. (2018). *Kantian ethics almost without apology.* Cornell University Press.

Black, W., & Living, R. (2004). Volunteerism as an occupation and its relationship to health and wellbeing. *British Journal of Occupational Therapy, 67*(12), 526–532.

Bono, G., Emmons, R. A., & McCullough, M. E. (2004). Gratitude in practice and the practice of gratitude. In P. A. Linley & S. Joseph (Eds.), *Positive psychology in practice* (pp. 464–481) Wiley.

Botes, A. (2000). A comparison between the ethics of justice and the ethics of care. *Journal of Advanced Nursing, 32*(5), 1071–1075.

Brown, M. F. (2008). Cultural relativism 2.0. *Current Anthropology, 49*(3), 363–383.

Bunge, M. (1989). *Ethics: The good and the right (Treatise on basic philosophy,* vol. 8). D. Reidel Publishing Company.

Caldecott, S. (2010). *Fruits of the spirit*. Catholic Truth Society.

Davis, D. E., Hook, J. N., Van Tongeren, D. R., Gartner, A. L., & Worthington, E. L., Jr. (2012). Can religion promote virtue?: A more stringent test of the model of relational spirituality and forgiveness. *International Journal for the Psychology of Religion, 22*(4), 252–266.

Davis, E. B., Plante, T. G., Grey, M. J., Kim, C. L., Freeman-Coppadge, D., Lefevor, G. T., Paulez, J. A., Giwa, S., Lasser, J., Stratton, S. P., Deneke, E., & Glowiak, K. J. (2021). The role of civility and cultural humility in navigating controversial areas in psychology. *Spirituality in Clinical Practice, 8*(2), 79–87.

Davis, J. H., Ruhe, J. A., Lee, M., & Rajadhyaksha, U. (2007). Mission possible: Do school mission statements work? *Journal of Business Ethics, 70*(1), 99–110.

DiFranks, N. N. (2008). Social workers and the NASW Code of Ethics: Belief, behavior, disjuncture. *Social Work, 53*(2), 167–176.

Emmons, R. A., & Crumpler, C. A. (2000). Gratitude as a human strength: Appraising the evidence. *Journal of social and clinical psychology, 19*(1), 56–69.

Emmons, R. A., & McCullough, M. E. (Eds.). (2004). *The psychology of gratitude*. Oxford University Press.

Enright, R. D. (2019). *Forgiveness is a choice: A step-by-step process for resolving anger and restoring hope*. American Psychological Association.

Feinberg, J. (2007). Psychological egoism. In R. Shafer-Landau, *Ethical theory: An anthology* (pp. 167–177). Blackwell.

Ghezzi, B. (1980). *The Angry Christian: How to control, and use, your anger*. Servant Books.

Gilbert, P. (Ed.). (2005). *Compassion: Conceptualisations, research and use in psychotherapy*. Routledge.

Healy, L. M. (2007). Universalism and cultural relativism in social work ethics. *International Social Work, 50*(1), 11–26.

Hollenbach, S. J., & Hollenbach, D. (2002). *The common good and Christian ethics*. Cambridge University Press.

Hursthouse, R. (1999). *On virtue ethics*. Oxford University Press.

Hutcheson, F. (2006). *A system of moral philosophy*. A&C Black.

Jos, P. H. (2006). Social contract theory: Implications for professional ethics. *American Review of Public Administration, 36*(2), 139–155.

Keating, T. (2000). *Fruits and gifts of the spirit*. Lantern Books.

Kelly, K. R. (2001). Introduction to the revised AMHCA Code of Ethics. *Journal of Mental Health Counseling, 23*(1), 1.

King, D. L., Case, C. J., & Premo, K. M. (2010). Current mission statement emphasis: Be ethical and go global. *Academy of Strategic Management Journal, 9*(2), 71.

Kirby, E. L., McBride, M. C., Shuler, S., Birkholt, M. J., Danielson, M. A., & Pawlowski, D. R. (2006). The Jesuit difference (?): Narratives of negotiating spiritual values and secular practices. *Communication Studies, 57*(1), 87–105.

*Knapp, S. J., VandeCreek, L. D., & Fingerhut, R. (2017). *Practical ethics for psychologists: A positive approach* (3rd ed.). American Psychological Association.

Korth, S. J. (2008). Precis of Ignatian pedagogy: A practical approach. In G. W. Traub, *A Jesuit education reader* (pp. 280–284). Loyola Press.

Lama, D. (2012). *Beyond religion: Ethics for a whole world*. Houghton Mifflin.

Manney, J. (2011). *A simple, life-changing prayer: Discovering the power of St. Ignatius Loyola's Examen*. Loyola Press.

McKinney, R. H. (2009). The Jesuit *magis* and the ethics of *ceteris paribus*. *International Philosophical Quarterly, 49*(1), 71–87.

Mescher, M. (2018). Teaching magis at college: Meaning, mission, and moral responsibility. *Jesuit Higher Education: A Journal, 7*(2), 4.

Muldoon, R. (2016). *Social contract theory for a diverse world: Beyond tolerance*. Routledge.

Nielsen, K. (1990). *Ethics without God* (rev. ed.). Prometheus Books.

Plante, T. G. (1995). Training child clinical predoctoral interns and postdoctoral fellows in ethics and professional issues: An experiential model. *Professional Psychology: Research and Practice, 26*(6), 616–619.

Plante, T. G. (1998). Teaching a course on psychology ethics to undergraduates: An experiential model. *Teaching of Psychology, 25*(4), 286–287.

Plante, T. G. (2004). *Do the right thing: Living ethically in an unethical world*. New Harbinger.

Plante, T. G. (Ed.). (2015). *The psychology of compassion and cruelty: Understanding the emotional, spiritual, and religious influences*. Praeger/ABC-CLIO.

Plante, T. G., & Pistoresi, S. (2017). A survey of ethics training in undergraduate psychology programs at Jesuit universities. *Pastoral Psychology, 66*, 353–358.

Plante, T. G., & Plante, L. G. (2017). *Graduating with honor: Best practices to promote ethics development in college students.* Praeger/ABC-CLIO.

Rachels, J., & Rachels, S. (2012). *The elements of moral philosophy* (7th ed.). McGraw-Hill.

Rash, J. A., Matsuba, M. K., & Prkachin, K. M. (2011). Gratitude and well-being: Who benefits the most from a gratitude intervention? *Applied Psychology: Health and Well-Being, 3*(3), 350–369.

Rezek, J., Cano, G., & Evans, B. (2011). Life, liberty and the pursuit of happiness: A Jeffersonian approach to development indicators. *American Economist, 56*(2), 35–46.

Scarre, G. (2020). *Utilitarianism.* Routledge.

Sia, S. (2008). Ethics and religion. *New Blackfriars, 89*(1024), 702–709.

Stern, R. (2015). *Kantian ethics: Value, agency, and obligation.* Oxford University Press.

Trianosky, G. (1990). What is virtue ethics all about? *American Philosophical Quarterly, 27*(4), 335–344.

Vaughn, L. (2015). *Beginning ethics: An introduction to moral philosophy.* Norton.

Vlastos, G. (1991). *Socrates, ironist and moral philosopher.* Cornell University Press.

Worthington, E. L., Jr. (Ed.). (2007). *Handbook of forgiveness.* Routledge.

Worthington, E. L., Jr. (2013). *Forgiveness and reconciliation: Theory and application.* Routledge.

Young, G. (2017). *Revising the APA ethics code.* Springer.

CHAPTER 9

Additional Spiritually Informed Life Principle Techniques and Principles

All the spiritual and religious traditions have much to offer in our efforts to understand and use elements of these great wisdom traditions in our contemporary lives. One book alone could certainly not do justice to what these traditions have to offer. The earlier chapters in this book highlight specific and unique contributions of Jesuit spirituality (e.g., the Examen, the 4 Ds of discernment, *curia personalis*). In this chapter, we will review a variety of principles and techniques that are more commonly found in numerous, if not all, the major religious and spiritual traditions. They can all be used, secularized, and incorporated into spiritually informed life principles. Thus, these approaches do not necessarily originate with Jesuit spirituality but are more commonly found within multiple religious and spiritual communities, as well as the core values of many secular individuals and cultures. All of them can be easily adapted in ways that can be used in secular-based society and living. They also can be adapted in ways that fit diverse religious and spiritual traditions and communities. This is not an exhaustive list by any means but also serves as a few primary examples that are common among the various spiritual and religious communities.

Prayer and Meditation

Prayer and meditative practices can be found in all the various spiritual and religious traditions. There is an enormous amount of research that has demonstrated the psychological and even physical health benefits of engaging in prayer and meditative practices (e.g., Imamoğlu & Dilek, 2016; McCullough, 1995; Spilka & Ladd, 2012). Many of these approaches have been adapted to appeal to diverse audiences including completely secular ones. Mindfulness is perhaps the best example of these efforts (e.g., Gilbert & Waltz, 2010; Hülsheger et al., 2013; Prazak et al., 2012). While mindfulness originated from the Buddhist tradition, it has been adapted and secularized in a way that appeals to a broad and diverse array of people (Brazier, 2013; Trammel, 2017). Mindfulness-based stress reduction is commonly offered in hospitals, clinics, universities, businesses, schools, and private practices (Grossman et al., 2004; Kabat-Zinn, 2003; Praissman, 2008). Research on mindfulness has exploded with many studies demonstrating the effectiveness of the practice on a wide range of issues and concerns (Baer et al., 2020; Creswell, 2017; Zhang et al., 2021).

Mindfulness is not the only meditative practice that is available, but it is the one that is the most readily recognized and practiced in recent decades (Bristow, 2019; Cayoun et al., 2018; Van Doesum et al., 2021). Other meditative and contemplative practices such as transcendental meditation, centering prayer, yoga, and so forth are also popular and can easily be integrated into psychotherapy (La Torre, 2001; Shapiro & Walsh, 2017; Walsh & Shapiro, 2006).

Case Example 9.1 Chloe

Chloe struggles from insomnia and anxiety. She often finds herself falling asleep without trouble, but then she wakes up in the middle of the night worrying and has trouble getting back to sleep. Her doctor reviewed common sleep hygiene recommendations, such as avoiding caffeine in the evening, not using her bed for activities other than sleeping (e.g., eating, watching television), reading calming materials before bed, shutting down her computer and phone before bedtime, taking a warm bath before bed, and other evidence-based best practices and strategies that promote a good night's sleep. Since Chloe is an engaged and practicing Catholic, she was encouraged to recite the Our Father and Hail Mary prayers when she woke up to calm her anxieties and to distract her from her worries. She found these prayers soothing, consoling, and helpful in getting back to sleep.

Case Example 9.2 Larry

Larry struggles with alcohol problems. After being fired from his job due to his addiction and resulting poor job performance, he joined Alcoholics Anonymous (AA). He is not very religious or spiritually minded, but he finds the 12 steps of AA a helpful structure for him. Additionally, the recitation of the Serenity Prayer (i.e., "God grant me the serenity to accept the things I cannot change, courage to change the things I can, and the wisdom to know the difference") at the meetings have been helpful to him as well. He experiences this recitation as not only a prayer but also as a thoughtful philosophy of life that he fully embraces. He puts a copy of the Serenity Prayer in his kitchen and recites it before each meal. He finds that the prayer helps to keep him grounded and centered throughout his day.

Exercise 9.1 Prayer and Meditation in Your Life

Do you pray or engage in a meditative process?

_____

There are many different approaches to both. What is your prayer or meditative approach like?

_____

_____

_____

Is it helpful?

_____

Could it be more helpful?

_____

What next steps might you be willing to do to better utilize prayer and meditation in your life?

_____

_____

Can you execute this plan? Why or why not?

_____

_____

_____

Meaning, Purpose, and Calling

All the religious and spiritual traditions offer reflection and wisdom about meaning, purpose, and calling in life (Emmons, 2005; Gould, 2011; Löwith, 2011). They attempt to offer suggestions about what really matters and have helpful strategies to deal with the common existential challenges many people experience when they feel lost or unmoored in life. Much research has focused on the psychological and physical benefits of finding meaning and purpose in life, and the spiritual and religious traditions offer much to help answer these questions in a thoughtful manner (Emmons, 2003; Park, 2005).

Case Example 9.3 Ben

Ben is active in his synagogue and feels that his Jewish tradition organizes and centers his life. His maternal grandparents were Holocaust survivors and instilled in Ben and his siblings the importance of holding onto their Jewish customs, practices, and identities. Ben embraces the _Tikkun olam_ notion of "repair the world" and is active in various charitable arms of his synagogue and community. Ben tries to keep his life balanced between his efforts to pursue his calling and the practicalities of earning a living and managing a large family with his wife and four children.

Case Example 9.4 Tran

Tran came to the United States after the conclusion of the Vietnam War in the 1970s as a young child. After a year in a refugee camp, she found her way with her family to a community in northern California where there was a large Vietnamese population. Tran and her family felt blessed by God in how they were able to survive the war and find their way to safety in the United States. After completing her education, Tran decided to dedicate her life to helping other refugees transition to the United States from challenging locations and situations. She went to law school and became an immigration lawyer. She works at a firm that focuses on "faith that does justice" and integrates faith with their legal activities and advocacy. She finds meaning and purpose in her life and feels that she is doing God's work.

Exercise 9.2 Meaning and Purpose in Your Life

What gives you meaning and purpose in your life?

_____

If you were on your deathbed with only hours to live, what would you think about as you review and reflect upon your life?

_____

_____

Write down the top five most important life purposes you have.

List Your Five Most Important Life Purposes

1. _____

2. _____

3. _____

4. _____

5. _____

Are you satisfied with your progress regarding these interests? Why or why not?

_____

_____

_____

Rituals and Community Events

Spiritual and religious traditions offer a great deal when it comes to rituals and community engagement and events (Graham & Haidt, 2010; McCauley & Lawson, 2002). Research indicates that rituals are important for human flourishing and overall ability to cope with life stressors (Bulbulia, 2004; Sosis, 2004). These diverse traditions offer much to choose from when it comes to rituals. Rituals might include daily or weekly practices (e.g., prayer, meditation, attending services, confession) but also those associated with major life events such as births, deaths, coming of age, marriage, and so forth.

Case Example 9.5   Susan

Susan lost her husband suddenly after he suffered an unexpected heart attack. She was devastated and felt completely in shock. She could barely speak or function. She was active in her Jewish community and once her synagogue was contacted, the staff immediately mobilized in getting funeral arrangements completed, organizing daily Shiva (i.e., a week of mourning rituals), and lining up people in the community to provide "mitzvah meals" for the next month. Her rabbi was helpful and consoling. Susan was encouraged to fully embrace the rituals and offerings of her tradition and synagogue so that she could more easily be on automatic pilot and accept much needed support during her difficult crisis and mourning period.

Case Example 9.6   Bob and Cathy

Bob and Cathy are retired and their adult children all live far away in other states. They have always been involved with their local Baptist church and since retirement, they have time to attend many of the church activities including Bible classes, study groups, and religious services. They decide to get even more involved with their church community and to volunteer for some of the charitable activities offered, such as the vacation Bible school program. They enjoy the work but also the social connections and various community engagement these experiences offer.

Exercise 9.3   Rituals and Community in Your Life

Are you part of a satisfying community?

_____

If not, why not?

_____

Do you engage in rituals that give you comfort and connection with others?

_____

Again, why or why not?

_____

Can you increase your community engagement for social support?

_____

What could you do to get more out of community involvement?

_____

Volunteerism

All the spiritual and religious traditions have ways to engage in volunteerism. Of course, a vast array of secular groups also offer compelling volunteer opportunities. Volunteerism has been found to be associated with both psychological and physical health benefits, including longevity (Jenkinson et al., 2013; Lum & Lightfoot, 2005; Piliavin & Siegl, 2007). Faith communities tend to be well organized for volunteerism with readily available programs and activities for those who wish to donate their time and efforts for the benefit of others (Lim & MacGregor, 2012; Lodi-Smith & Roberts, 2007). Examples include soup kitchens, homeless shelters, mission trips, food banks and food pantries, visiting the sick and infirm, and helping challenged children or the elderly. Religious communities as well as many secular organizations have these services very well organized and structured with often a national or global reach (Ruiter & De Graaf, 2006).

Case Example 9.7 Xavier

Xavier is a recently retired man who never married and never had children. He was an only child, so he has no siblings, nieces, or nephews. His parents have passed away. He feels very much alone in the world, and he feels lonely and depressed. He is not a religious man, but he felt comfortable with the Episcopalian Church since he grew up in the Anglican Church while living in England as a youth. The local Episcopalian Church has a vibrant ministry to provide food for shut-ins and the homeless too. Xavier decided to volunteer with the program and was quickly very busy with this ministry. He developed close relationships with fellow volunteers and got to know many of the clientele that the ministry was serving. His depression and loneliness subsided as he became more fully engaged and invested in this important volunteer ministry.

Case Example 9.8 Maki

Maki is a high school student interested in attending the school's immersion trip to Mexico during the upcoming spring break where the group will assist in building homes in a rural and isolated area of the country. Many of her friends are going on the trip, and she believes it will be a good way to spend time with her friends during the upcoming spring break. Once there, she connects with some local families who have hosted the group and quickly learns of the challenges of rural life in that part of the country. After returning to the United States, she signs up for a more extensive volunteer trip during the summer to Guatemala where she thrives. She feels like she gets out of her own concerns and troubles focusing on the challenges of the people she is working with abroad. She feels like her personal concerns become more of a background noise when she is working to help others.

Exercise 9.4 Volunteerism and You

Do you engage in volunteerism on a regular basis? If so, what do you do and how does it impact you?

_____

_____

If you do not engage in volunteerism, what holds you back?

_____

Would you consider starting a volunteer activity?

_____

If so, what interests you in volunteerism?

_____

What would your next steps be to pursue this interest?

_____

_____

Can you do it soon? Why or why not?

_____

_____

_____

Social Justice

Spiritual and religious traditions have much to offer regarding social justice activities as well (McCracken, 2014; Rausch, 2010; Wood, 2002). These priorities and interests are often connected to their volunteer activities and opportunities. Social justice efforts typically attempt to advocate for and assist those who are on the margins of society (e.g., the poor, displaced, minorities) and provide meaning and purpose to those engaged in these activities and advocacy efforts (Dinter, 2022; Opongo & Orobator, 2007; Rausch, 2010). Social justice tries to make the community and world more humane and just. Young people, in particular, find that social justice activities and priorities are what keeps them connected to and affiliated with religious communities and traditions (Bergman, 2011; Rausch, 2010).

Case Example 9.9 Aislin

Aislin is a college student who is undocumented. Her parents left El Salvador when she was only two years old and came to the United States illegally. Aislin has been able to negotiate her education and life in the United States pretty well, but she does not have a driver's license, Social Security number, and so forth. She is an excellent student and an extremely likable person. Teachers, coaches, clerics, and others have tried to help her find a path to success. Although she gets discouraged and anxious at times, she is coping well. She is interested in social justice advocacy through her church to help refugees and others stranded at the U.S.-Mexico border. She has made several trips there and comes back more energized and motivated to help further. She felt that she might be able to help others who are in circumstances like her own, which gives her feelings of empowerment and purpose.

Case Example 9.10 Chi

Chi lost his younger brother to suicide while his brother was in college. Chi was devastated, as he and his brother were close. Chi felt terrible grief and depression from his loss. Chi decides to get involved with advocacy for student mental health on college campuses hoping that he might contribute to saving lives in the future. His Buddhist temple is supportive of his efforts and agrees to collaborate with him in these efforts. Others from his temple are enlisted as they work to advocate for better mental health services for students in his local area.

Exercise 9.5 Social Justice and You

Are you interested in social justice?

_____

Why or why not?

_____

Is there an important cause or group of marginalized people that especially interest you?

_____

Why or why not?

_____

_____

_____

Spiritual Models

Much research has been conducted and published on social or observational learning Bandura et al., 1966; Pratt et al., 2010). We often model our behavior after those high status or important models in our lives that could parents, grandparents, teachers, coaches, and clerics but also could include famous global models such as Jesus, Mother Teresa, Martin Luther King, Gandhi, Nelson Mandela, and so forth (Bandura, 2003; Oman & Thoresen, 2003). These models provide inspiration to those who value their ideals and accomplishments and can help us to nurture certain highly valued traits and characteristics (Oman et al., 2012).

Case Example 9.11 Jerry

Jerry was very close to his grandfather, Henry. Henry was a religious man who was kind and gentle. He never seemed to have a bad word to say about anyone and he would sprinkle his conversations with biblical quotes in what appeared to be an honest and humble manner. As Jerry aged and long after his grandfather's death, Jerry wanted to emulate him in how he interacted with others and how he maintained a positive outlook.

Case Example 9.12 Bo

Bo has always admired the Dalai Lama and has read all his books and other materials about his life. He was thrilled to meet the Dalai Lama briefly during one of his visits at a local university. Bo was especially impressed with the Dalai Lama's emphasis on compassion and his lightheartedness too. Bo was struggling with some coworker-related difficulties and used the Dalai Lama as a model for how to be more compassionate to others and less dragged down by interpersonal tensions.

Exercise 9.6 Spiritual Models in Your Life

Do you have someone in your life who you emulate as a spiritual model? If so, who are they, and what is it about them that impresses and influences you?

_____

_____

If not, are there people in your life, known or people you have never met, who have really impressed you as people you would want to emulate? If so, what is it about them that you relate to and are impressed by?

How can you alter your behavior to be more like them?

Being Part of Something Bigger Than Oneself

The spiritual and religious communities offer us the opportunity to be part of something bigger and grander than ourselves (Hattie & Beagan, 2013; Kinnvall, 2004). They provide an identity for many and a community of like-minded people interested in many similar interests, beliefs, and practices (Markstrom-Adams et al., 1994). Certainly, being part of something grander and larger than ourselves does not need to be exclusive to religious and spiritual communities, but it might include sport teams, hobbies, or university affiliations. Yet, the spiritual and religious traditions are centuries old and help many feel part of something that is stable, multigenerational, and eternal (Oppong, 2013).

Case Example 9.13 Bill

Bill is close to retirement and tends to feel lonely and undervalued as he feels that younger people no longer appreciate his business skills and other assets. He decides to teach business at a local faith-based college as an adjunct professor and really identifies with the university and its faith-based mission. He attends most of the sporting events and campus lectures and although he is a recent adjunct, he feels very much accepted by everyone. He feels part of something bigger and feels connected to his new university community. The faith element of the school makes him feel that he is part of something important that extends past the college's campus.

Case Example 9.14 Lori

Lori is not especially religious but feels part of the Jewish community. She attends services at her local temple and feels that she is with family there. The music, language, and traditions speak to her in ways that nothing else does. When she feels depressed, anxious, and upset about things, she attends services at her temple and feels held in the community, warmth, and traditions there.

Exercise 9.7 Being Part of Something Bigger in Your Life

Do you feel part of something bigger than yourself in your life? Perhaps it might be a cause, a religious or spiritual tradition or community, a sports team, an identity group, a political affiliation, or a profession?

_____

What makes you feel part of something bigger in your life?

_____

How does this help you?

_____

_____

_____

_____

Bibliotherapy

The spiritual and religious communities offer a great deal to read (Griffiths, 1999). Reading materials might include sacred scripture (e.g., the Bible, Koran, Talmud) or may include commentary on scripture and on the various aspects, beliefs, practices, and wisdom of the religious traditions (Dewi & Widiyanti, 2018). Additionally, more contemporary reading from the various spiritual and religious traditions focuses on ways to use the wisdom from these traditions for better living (Bálint & Magyari, 2020; Jack & Ronan, 2008).

Case Example 9.15 Andre

Andre enjoys many different contemplative practices from various spiritual and religious traditions. He likes to try different ones to determine which might become his favorites or which ones to use in certain circumstances. One of his daily traditions is *Lectio Divina*, a meditative practice of reading sacred text (Robertson, 2011). It includes four steps—read, meditate, pray, and contemplate (Gray, 2014). Andre has been stressed lately and uses the *Lectio Divina* process as a way of coping.

Case Example 9.16 Donna

Donna enjoys various meditative practices from the Buddhist tradition, including passage meditation developed by Eknath Easwaran (Easwaran, 2010; Oman et al., 2006). She does a daily reading of an inspiring and consoling text and memorizes it. She repeats and reflects on the text for about 20 minutes in the morning before she begins her day. She finds that it helps to organize and center her before she begins her busy and often stressful day.

Exercise 9.8 Bibliotherapy and You?

What do you like to read? Are there readings that help you feel relaxed, inspired, energized? If so, what are they?

_____

_____

If not, would you be willing to start a reading habit in this way?

_____

Where would you go for ideas to develop your reading list?

_____

_____

_____

Conclusion

The spiritual and religious communities have much to offer to enhance our lives, regardless of our own beliefs, practices, and traditions. These approaches can be adapted to use with diverse people, including those who are not interested in or affiliated with any religious or spiritual tradition. They provide value-added approaches and tools to general evidence-based best practices in managing our lives.

Further Reading

Bergman, R. C. (2011). *Catholic social learning: Educating the faith that does justice.* Fordham University Press.

Dinter, P. E. (2022). *This I believe: A faith that does justice.* Wipf and Stock Publishers.

Easwaran, E. (2010). *Passage meditation: Bringing the deep wisdom of the heart into daily life* (3rd ed.). Nilgiri Press.

Fiala, A. (2007). *What would Jesus really do?: The power and limits of Jesus' moral teachings.* Rowman & Littlefield Publishers.

Gray, T. (2014). *Praying scripture for a change: An introduction to Lectio Divina.* Ascension Press.

Griffiths, P. J. (1999). *Religious reading: The place of reading in the practice of religion.* Oxford University Press.

Kabat-Zinn, J. (2003). Mindfulness-based stress reduction (MBSR). *Constructivism in the Human Sciences, 8*(2), 73–107.

McCauley, R. N., & Lawson, E. T. (2002). *Bringing ritual to mind: Psychological foundations of cultural forms.* Cambridge University Press.

McCracken, V. (Ed.). (2014). *Christian faith and social justice: Five views.* A&C Black.

Robertson, D. (2011). *Lectio Divina: The medieval experience of reading.* Liturgical Press.

Shapiro, D. H., & Walsh, R. N. (Eds.). (2017). *Meditation: Classic and contemporary perspectives.* Routledge.

Spilka, B., & Ladd, K. L. (2012). *The psychology of prayer: A scientific approach.* Guilford Press.

Wood, R. L. (2002). *Faith in action: Religion, race, and democratic organizing in America.* University of Chicago Press.

References

Baer, R., Caldera, C., & Nagy, L. M. (2020). Mindfulness. In V. Zeigler-Hill & T. K. Shackelford (Eds.), *Encyclopedia of Personality and Individual Differences* (pp. 2898–2908). Springer.

Bálint, Á., & Magyari, J. (2020). The use of bibliotherapy in revealing and addressing the spiritual needs of cancer patients. *Religions, 11*(3), 128.

Bandura, A. (2003). On the psychosocial impact and mechanisms of spiritual modeling: Comment. *International Journal for the Psychology of Religion, 13*(3), 167–173.

Bandura, A., Grusec, J. E., & Menlove, F. L. (1966). Observational learning as a function of symbolization and incentive set. *Child development, 37*(3), 499–506.

Bergman, R. C. (2011). *Catholic social learning: Educating the faith that does justice.* Fordham University Press.

Brazier, C. (2013). Roots of mindfulness. *European Journal of Psychotherapy & Counselling, 15*(2), 127–138.

Bristow, J. (2019). Mindfulness in politics and public policy. *Current Opinion in Psychology, 28*, 87–91.

Bulbulia, J. (2004). The cognitive and evolutionary psychology of religion. *Biology and philosophy, 19*(5), 655–686.

Cayoun, B. A., Francis, S. E., & Shires, A. G. (2018). *The clinical handbook of mindfulness-integrated cognitive behavior therapy: A step-by-step guide for therapists.* John Wiley & Sons.

Creswell, J. D. (2017). Mindfulness interventions. *Annual review of psychology, 68*(1), 491–516.

Dewi, I. P., & Widiyanti, A. T. (2018). Qur'anic therapy (Islamic bibliotherapy) to improve religious coping in hemodialysis patients. *Media Keperawatan Indonesia, 1*(3), 12–17.

Dinter, P. E. (2022). *This I believe: A faith that does justice.* Wipf and Stock Publishers.

Easwaran, E. (2010). *Passage meditation: Bringing the deep wisdom of the heart into daily life* (3rd ed.). Niligiri Press.

Emmons, R. A. (2003). *The psychology of ultimate concerns: Motivation and spirituality in personality.* Guilford Press.

Emmons, R. A. (2005). Striving for the sacred: Personal goals, life meaning, and religion. *Journal of Social Issues, 61*(4), 731–745.

Gilbert, D., & Waltz, J. (2010). Mindfulness and health behaviors. *Mindfulness, 1*(4), 227–234.

Gould, S. J. (2011). *Rocks of ages: Science and religion in the fullness of life.* Ballantine Books.

Graham, J., & Haidt, J. (2010). Beyond beliefs: Religions bind individuals into moral communities. *Personality and social psychology review, 14*(1), 140–150.

Gray, T. (2014). *Praying scripture for a change: An introduction to Lectio Divina.* Ascension Press.

Griffiths, P. J. (1999). *Religious reading: The place of reading in the practice of religion.* Oxford University Press.

Grossman, P., Niemann, L., Schmidt, S., & Walach, H. (2004). Mindfulness-based stress reduction and health benefits: A meta-analysis. *Journal of Psychosomatic Research, 57*(1), 35–43.

Hattie, B., & Beagan, B. L. (2013). Reconfiguring spirituality and sexual/gender identity: "It's a feeling of connection to something bigger, it's part of a wholeness." *Journal of Religion & Spirituality in Social Work: Social Thought, 32*(3), 244–268.

Hülsheger, U. R., Alberts, H. J. E. M., Feinholdt, A., & Lang, J. W. B. (2013). Benefits of mindfulness at work: the role of mindfulness in emotion regulation, emotional exhaustion, and job satisfaction. *Journal of Applied Psychology, 98*(2), 310–325.

Imamoğlu, O., & Dilek, A. N. (2016). Common benefits of prayer and yoga on human organism. *International Journal of Sport Culture and Science, 4*(Special Issue 2), 639–651.

Jack, S. J., & Ronan, K. R. (2008). Bibliotherapy: Practice and research. *School Psychology International, 29*(2), 161–182.

Jenkinson, C. E., Dickens, A. P., Jones, K., Thompson-Coon, J., Taylor, R. S., Rogers, M., Bambra, C. L., Lang, I., & Richards, S. H. (2013). Is volunteering a public health intervention? A systematic review and meta-analysis of the health and survival of volunteers. *BMC public health, 13*(1), 773.

Kabat-Zinn, J. (2003). Mindfulness-based stress reduction (MBSR). *Constructivism in the Human Sciences, 8*(2), 73–107.

Kinnvall, C. (2004). Globalization and religious nationalism: Self, identity, and the search for ontological security. *Political Psychology, 25*(5), 741–767.

La Torre, M. A. (2001). Meditation and psychotherapy: An effective combination. *Perspectives in Psychiatric Care, 37*(3), 103–106.

Lim, C., & MacGregor, C. A. (2012). Religion and volunteering in context: Disentangling the contextual effects of religion on voluntary behavior. *American Sociological Review, 77*(5), 747–779.

Lodi-Smith, J., & Roberts, B. W. (2007). Social investment and personality: A meta-analysis of the relationship of personality traits to investment in work, family, religion, and volunteerism. *Personality and Social Psychology Review, 11*(1), 68–86.

Löwith, K. (2011). *Meaning in history: The theological implications of the philosophy of history.* University of Chicago Press.

Lum, T. Y., & Lightfoot, E. (2005). The effects of volunteering on the physical and mental health of older people. *Research on aging, 27*(1), 31–55.

Markstrom-Adams, C., Hofstra, G., & Dougher, K. (1994). The ego-virtue of fidelity: A case for the study of religion and identity formation in adolescence. *Journal of Youth and Adolescence, 23*(4), 453–469.

McCauley, R. N., & Lawson, E. T. (2002). *Bringing ritual to mind: Psychological foundations of cultural forms.* Cambridge University Press.

McCracken, V. (Ed.). (2014). *Christian faith and social justice: Five views.* A&C Black.

McCullough, M. E. (1995). Prayer and health: Conceptual issues, research review, and research agenda. *Journal of Psychology and Theology, 23*(1), 15–29.

Oman, D., Hedberg, J., & Thoresen, C. E. (2006). Passage meditation reduces perceived stress in health professionals: A randomized, controlled trial. *Journal of Consulting and Clinical Psychology, 74*(4), 714–719.

Oman, D., & Thoresen, C. E. (2003). Spiritual modeling: A key to spiritual and religious growth? *International Journal for the Psychology of Religion, 13*(3), 149–165.

Oman, D., Thoresen, C. E., Park, C. L., Shaver, P. R., Hood, R. W., & Plante, T. G. (2012). Spiritual modeling self-efficacy. *Psychology of Religion and Spirituality, 4*(4), 278–297.

Opongo, E. O., & Orobator, A. E. (2007). *Faith doing justice.* Paulines Publications Africa.

Oppong, S. H. (2013). Religion and identity. *American International Journal of Contemporary Research, 3*(6), 10–16.

Park, C. L. (2005). Religion as a meaning-making framework in coping with life stress. *Journal of Social Issues, 61*(4), 707–729.

Piliavin, J. A., & Siegl, E. (2007). Health benefits of volunteering in the Wisconsin longitudinal study. *Journal of Health and Social Behavior, 48*(4), 450–464.

Praissman, S. (2008). Mindfulness-based stress reduction: A literature review and clinician's guide. *Journal of the American Academy of Nurse Practitioners, 20*(4), 212–216.

Pratt, T. C., Cullen, F. T., Sellers, C. S., Winfree L. T., Jr., Madensen, T. D., Daigle, L. E., Fearn, N. E., & Gau, J. M. (2010). The empirical status of social learning theory: A meta-analysis. *Justice Quarterly, 27*(6), 765–802.

Prazak, M., Critelli, J., Martin, L., Miranda, V., Purdum, M., & Powers, C. (2012). Mindfulness and its role in physical and psychological health. *Applied Psychology: Health and Well-Being, 4*(1), 91–105.

Rausch, T. P. (2010). *Educating for faith and justice: Catholic higher education today.* Liturgical Press.

Robertson, D. (2011). *Lectio Divina: The medieval experience of reading.* Liturgical Press.

Ruiter, S., & De Graaf, N. D. (2006). National context, religiosity, and volunteering: Results from 53 countries. *American Sociological Review, 71*(2), 191–210.

Shapiro, D. H., & Walsh, R. N. (Eds.). (2017). *Meditation: Classic and contemporary perspectives.* Routledge.

Sosis, R. (2004). The adaptive value of religious ritual: Rituals promote group cohesion by requiring members to engage in behavior that is too costly to fake. *American Scientist, 92*(2), 166–172.

Spilka, B., & Ladd, K. L. (2012). *The psychology of prayer: A scientific approach.* Guilford Press.

*Trammel, R. C. (2017). Tracing the roots of mindfulness: Transcendence in Buddhism and Christianity. *Journal of Religion & Spirituality in Social Work: Social Thought, 36*(3), 367–383.

Van Doesum, N. J., Murphy, R. O., Gallucci, M., Aharonov-Majar, E., Athenstaedt, U., Au, W. T., ... & Van Lange, P. A. M. (2021). Social mindfulness and prosociality vary across the globe. *Proceedings of the National Academy of Sciences, 118*(35), e2023846118.

Walsh, R., & Shapiro, S. L. (2006). The meeting of meditative disciplines and Western psychology: A mutually enriching dialogue. *American Psychologist, 61*(3), 227–239.

Wood, R. L. (2002). *Faith in action: Religion, race, and democratic organizing in America.* University of Chicago Press.

Zhang, D., Lee, E. K. P., Mak, E. C. W., Ho, C. Y., & Wong, S. Y. S. (2021). Mindfulness-based interventions: An overall review. *British Medical Bulletin, 138*(1), 41–57.

CHAPTER 10

Conclusions and Next Steps

I hope that by reading this book, you now have a better understanding and appreciation for spiritually informed life principles, strategies, and wisdom that Jesuit spirituality, in particular, and other spiritual and religious traditions more generally have to offer. These important and influential wisdom traditions have been perfecting their reflections on the many difficult challenges of human behavior and relationships long before anyone ever heard of or practiced psychotherapy. We have much to learn from these traditions. Many secular people are simply uninformed or even resistant to learning about what these wisdom traditions have to offer. Sadly, too many recoil from anything that has to do with religion. While some spiritually rooted strategies and interventions have been embraced and practiced in a secular manner (e.g., mindfulness meditation, yoga), many others have not.

While it is beyond the scope of this book, or any book, to fully review what all the spiritual and religious traditions offer us, this book seeks to highlight the strategies that are based on Jesuit spirituality. The fact that the Jesuits operate 27 colleges and universities in the United States and about 150 globally (worth also mentioning Jesuit elementary and high schools too) means that Jesuit higher education impacts numerous people both nationally and globally. Their influence is found in higher education where many students could potentially benefit from their wisdom for living, which is consistent with the mission and identity of their colleges and universities.

Potential life-enhancing strategies, such as the use of the Examen, using the four *D*s of discernment, treating each other with a *cura personalis* perspective, looking for the divine and the sacred in all, and so forth, can all be included in our life management toolbox. These value-added tools can be used and integrated with the arsenal of other tools commonly employed in coping with life stressors and our efforts to thrive and flourish. The tools and strategies offered in this book can be used as needed or desired by anyone regardless of their interest, or lack of interest, in spirituality and religion.

It is important to note that reading a book about spiritually informed life principles may be helpful but is not sufficient in our efforts to thrive and flourish. It is a start but not the completion of learning and growth. There is much more to do in order to get the most out of life (e.g., exercise, social support, meaningful work). In this final chapter, it is important to look to the future of this area of spiritually informed life principles as well as outline ways to increase our skills. Therefore, let me address next steps and strategies for taking this all on the road.

Future Directions

Frankly, spiritual and religious traditions and strategies have been rather late to the research and evidence-based party. Too often these approaches have been used in settings that were not as interested in the highest quality of empirical support. Although many of these approaches and interventions have been available for centuries, it has only been in recent years that they have been subject to randomized clinical trials. Not surprisingly, mindfulness likely has the most research support since it has become so popular, at least in the United States, since about the year 2000 (Brown et al., 2007). Empirical research support for mindfulness exploded around the year 2007 and afterwards with numerous studies conducted across the globe (Langer, 2014; Zhang et al., 2021). In more recent years, research on yoga has started to take off as well (Ciezar-Andersen et al., 2020; Dutta et al., 2022). Other approaches, including many that have been discussed in this book, are only recently getting interest from researchers. For example, the Examen has been subject to research studies, including randomized trials, only very recently (Plante, 2021). Therefore, much more research is needed to fully evaluate the usefulness of spiritually informed life principles. This research will take time and effort, and so we must do the best that we can with the available data now until this important research is completed and published. We need to have this research conducted so that we will have more confidence in knowing that these approaches work.

In the meantime, we cannot wait for research to be completed as we try to use all the tools readily available to us to help ourselves live better now. We must act with the best available data but proceed with caution. For those interested in perusing spiritually informed life principles, there is much that can be done to improve our skills. Here are a few strategies for next steps with learning more.

Next Steps: Taking It on the Road
1. Some Further Reading

There are a number of empirically based books that have been published introducing, explaining, and demonstrating spiritually informed life principles. Thus, there is much to choose from in terms of further reading. To get started, you might consider looking at some of the following:

Land, H. (2015). *Spirituality, religion, and faith in psychotherapy: Evidence-based expressive methods for mind, brain, and body*. Lyceum Books.

Pargament, K. I. (2001). *The psychology of religion and coping: Theory, research, practice*. Guilford Press.

Pargament, K. I., & Exline, J. J. (2021). *Working with spiritual struggles in psychotherapy: From research to practice*. Guilford.

Plante, T. G. (Ed.). (2010). *Contemplative practices in action: Spirituality, meditation, and health*. Praeger/ABC-CLIO.

Plante, T. G. (Ed.). (2012). *Religion, spirituality, and positive psychology: Understanding the psychological fruits of faith*. Praeger/ABC-CLIO.

Plante, T. G. (Ed.). (2018). *Healing with spiritual practices: Proven techniques for disorders from addictions and anxiety to cancer and chronic pain*. Praeger/ABC-CLIO.

Worthington, E. L., Jr. (2009). *Forgiving and reconciling: Bridges to wholeness and hope*. InterVarsity Press.

Additionally, you may wish to read more about Jesuit history and spirituality. These books will help readers develop a better understanding and appreciation for Jesuit spirituality that is the foundation of the principles in this book. See below for some references.

Heider, D. (2019). Jesuit psychology and the theory of knowledge. In C. Casalini (Ed.), *Jesuit Philosophy on the Eve of Modernity* (pp. 115–134). Brill.

McGreevy, J. T. (2016). *American Jesuits and the world: How an embattled religious order made modern Catholicism global*. Princeton University Press.

Meissner, W. W. (1992). *Ignatius of Loyola: The psychology of a saint*. Yale University Press.

O'Malley, J. W. (1993). *The first Jesuits*. Harvard University Press.

O'Malley, J. W. (2014). *The Jesuits: a history from Ignatius to the present*. Rowman & Littlefield.

Worcester, T. (Ed.). (2008). *The Cambridge companion to the Jesuits*. Cambridge University Press.

Worcester, T. (Ed.). (2017). *The Cambridge encyclopedia of the Jesuits*. Cambridge University Press.

Županov, I. G. (Ed.). (2019). *The Oxford handbook of the Jesuits*. Oxford University Press.

2. Find a Spiritual Director

Retreat centers, Jesuit institutions (e.g., high schools, colleges and universities), and various spiritual and religious groups have mechanisms to find a spiritual director to help personally guide your path toward further reflection, learning, and skill development. You can contact these organizations, wherever you happen to live, to determine what opportunities are available in your local area.

3. Practice, Practice, Practice

It is one thing to read about and even participate in exercises as suggested in this book. It is quite another thing to *practice* these strategies and principles so that they become part of your daily routine. Perhaps you can make a sincere and proactive effort to keep practicing the various strategies and exercises outlined in this book. It is important to develop a program and pattern of practice that is completed daily and is sustainable. It should be incorporated into your everyday life so that it becomes a natural way to get through your day. Associating these practices with your daily routine (e.g., meals, bedtime rituals, exercise) may be helpful to maintain consistency. As the saying goes, "practice makes perfect."

4. Keep a Reminder of These Principles Handy

We all need reminders and perhaps keeping the principles discussed in this book as a reminder would be helpful. Perhaps paste this brief list below on your refrigerator, on your bathroom mirror, or at your workstation. A version you can easily tear out and use is provided at the end of this chapter.

Seven Principles of Spiritually Informed Life Principles

1 See God (or the sacred) in all things
2 Embrace *Cura personalis* (i.e., care for the whole person)
3 The four *D*s of discernment and decision making (i.e., discovery, detachment, discernment, direction)
4 Use the Examen as an end-of-day review, reflection, and prayer
5 Manage conflict with accommodation, humility, and the expectation of goodness
6 Travel the path to kinship with civility, hospitality, solidarity, and mutuality
7 Embrace ethical decision-making strategies

5. Follow Principles of Success

As we come to the end of this book, and this concluding chapter, it is important to offer suggestions regarding principles of success moving forward with incorporating spiritually informed life principles into your life. What follows is not an exhaustive list but simply a few principles to keep in mind as you complete this book and pursue these principles in your daily life.

Humility

When it comes to religion and spirituality, we always must be careful regarding those who seem to have all the answers yet none of the questions. Some seem to know it all and have no curiosity or interest in what they do not know. It is important to remain humble in this area especially when so many others may act in ways that suggest overconfidence. People can get very defensive about their particular brand of beliefs and interests in religion, spirituality, and life lessons, and you may find that some people are exceedingly overconfident. Humility in general, and cultural humility, in particular, are important qualities and virtues to maintain and will hopefully keep us all learning and growing in a rapidly developing yet sensitive area of life.

Evidence-Based Best Practices

It has become more important to keep track of and act on evidence-based best practices when they are available. This can often be accomplished by paying attention to the work of various professional organizations, institutions, books, and journals that specialize in these areas. It is important to be careful and thoughtful so that whatever spiritually informed life principles we plan to embrace are backed up by appropriate quality research and best practices. People have all sorts of ideas and suggestions that may have little, if any, empirical support. Of course, when quality research findings do not yet exist, we must proceed with great caution and thoughtful consideration doing the best that we can with whatever information we have to work with.

Keep Up with New Developments

New developments are hard to keep up with since there are so many journals, conferences, conventions, books, and new developments constantly emerging, especially in areas such as this one where the newness of the field makes for rapid and sometimes seismic growth and progress. We need to find reasonable and sustainable ways to keep up with these advances. Being thoughtful and proactive may help. Getting consultation and mentoring from experts can be invaluable too.

Conclusion

As we conclude this book, I hope that you will find a way to use these spiritually informed life principles and tools in your personal and professional lives in a way that is helpful, healing, and productive. The great wisdom traditions offer much to all of us when we reflect upon them and find ways to make their efforts work for us in contemporary times. As someone who has been working at a Jesuit university for over 30 years, I have been constantly amazed at the wisdom offered by Jesuit leaders and writers since the society was started over 500 years ago. While St. Ignatius, as an example, was not a psychotherapist, perhaps he could have been had he lived in modern times. We should not be afraid or resistant to ask important questions about these tools and to be sure that these tools work in practice. We always must follow good data where it leads and then apply them to our lives to live as well as we can. In doing so, we help to create a better world for ourselves and for others, and there are few things more important than doing so.

References

Brown, K. W., Ryan, R. M., & Creswell, J. D. (2007). Mindfulness: Theoretical foundations and evidence for its salutary effects. *Psychological Inquiry, 18*(4), 211–237.

Ciezar-Andersen, S. D., Hayden, K. A., & King-Shier, K. M. (2021). A systematic review of yoga interventions for helping health professionals and students. *Complementary Therapies in Medicine, 58*, 102704.

Dutta, A., Aruchunan, M., Mukherjee, A., Metri, K. G., Ghosh, K., & Basu-Ray, I. (2022). A comprehensive review of yoga research in 2020. *Journal of Integrative and Complementary Medicine, 28*(2), 114–123.

Langer, E. J. (2014). *Mindfulness.* Da Capo Lifelong Books.

lante, T. G. (2021). Using the Examen, a Jesuit prayer, in spiritually integrated and secular psychotherapy, *Pastoral Psychology, 71*, 119–125.

Zhang, D., Lee, E. K. P., Mak, E. C. W., Ho, C. Y., & Wong, S. Y. S. (2021). Mindfulness-based interventions: An overall review. *British Medical Bulletin, 138*(1), 41–57.

SEVEN PRINCIPLES OF SPIRITUALLY INFORMED LIFE PRINCIPLES

1. See God (or the sacred) in all things

2. Embrace *Cura personalis* (i.e., care for the whole person)

3. Use the four *D*s of discernment and decision making (i.e., discovery, detachment, discernment, direction)

4. Use the Examen for end-of-day review, reflection, and prayer

5. Manage conflict with accommodation, humility, and the expectation of goodness

6. Travel the path to kinship with civility, hospitality, solidarity, and mutuality

7. Embrace ethical decision-making strategies

Index

About the Author

Thomas G. Plante, Ph.D., ABPP is the Augustin Cardinal Bea, S.J., University Professor and a professor of psychology and, by courtesy, religious studies, as well as the director of the Applied Spirituality Institute at Santa Clara University. He is also an adjunct clinical professor of psychiatry and behavioral sciences at Stanford University School of Medicine. He is a fellow of the American Psychological Association (APA) and is the current editor of the APA journal *Spirituality in Clinical Practice*. He served as vice chair of the National Review Board for the Protection of Children and Youth for the United States Conference of Catholic Bishops (USCCB) and was the president of the Society for the Psychology of Religion and Spirituality (Division 36 of the APA). He has published over 250 professional journal articles and book chapters. Additionally, he has published 27 books, including: *Human Interaction with the Divine, the Sacred, and the Deceased: Psychological, Scientific, and Theological Perspectives* (2022); *Healing with Spiritual Practices: Proven Techniques for Disorders from Addictions and Anxiety to Cancer and Chronic Pain* (2018); *Graduating With Honor: Best Practices to Promote Ethics Development in College Students* (2017); *Do the Right Thing: Living Ethically in an Unethical World* (2004); *Sexual Abuse in the Catholic Church: A Decade of Crisis, 2002–2012* (2011); and *Spiritual Practices in Psychotherapy: Thirteen Tools for Enhancing Psychological Health* (2009). He has been featured in numerous media outlets, including *TIME Magazine, CNN, NBC Nightly News, The PBS News Hour, New York Times, USA Today, British Broadcasting Company*, and *National Public Radio*, among many others. He has evaluated or treated more than a thousand priests and applicants to the priesthood and diaconate and has served as a consultant for a number of Roman Catholic and Episcopal Church dioceses and religious orders. *TIME Magazine* referred to him (April 1, 2002) as one of "three leading (American) Catholics."